CHARLES COUNTY, MARYLAND

WILLS
1818-1825

Will Book HB-14

Abstracted by

Michael R. Marshall

Colonial Roots
Millsboro, DE
2015

Colonial
Roots

Helping you grow your family tree

ISBN 978-1-68034-026-6
Published January 2015

CONTENTS

[page intentionally blank]

INTRODUCTION

This book contains detailed abstracts, from Maryland Archives microfilm CR 49157-2, of the 174 wills that were recorded in Charles County, Maryland, during the years from 1818 to 1825.

Humphrey Barnes was the Register of Wills during this period.

An alphabetical will index begins on page 109, which lists the names of those whose wills are listed in this volume.

The general index contains the names of all persons and tracts of land mentioned in the 174 wills.

Notes with parenthesis "{ }" contain additional information or clarification.

Names are spelled as they appear. The most common usage was indexed.

Michael R. Marshall
January 2015

[page intentionally blank]

Charles County Maryland, Wills 1818-1825
Will Book HB-14

Page 1.

Patience Davis, Will, September 30, 1811; December 9, 1817

I, Patience Davis of CC, being sick and weak of body, but of sound mind, memory and understanding;

To daughter Sarah Ann, wife of Benjamin Burgess, the use of negroes, Cecy, Priscilla, William, Levanner, during her life and then to her children. Also the use of negro Sophia until {granddaughter} Sarah Ann Burgess arrives at age of 16 yrs or day of marriage.

Executor: son-in-law Benjamin Burgess

Signed: September 30, 1811   Patience Davis

Wit: James Davis, Frederick Nelson

Page 2.

Sarah Queen, Will, December 8, 1817; February 11, 1818

I, Sarah Queen of CC, being weak in body, but of sound mind and memory;

To nephew Marsham Bowling, negroes; Nan, Harry, Allen, Matthew, Hizey, Sarah and her daughters Celey and Teresa, Eliza and Ann, also my largest dining tables having eagle claws to the feet.

To nephew William Queen, negroes; Moses, Len, Pat, Monica and her son Francis, also 2nd largest dining table.

To niece Mary Gardiner, negro Rachel, the bed and furniture called the priest bed.

To nephew Samuel Queen, negro Alice.

To niece Eleanor Boarman wife of John, negro Agnes.

To niece Mary Ann Queen, negro Henny.

To niece Mary Bowling, negro Monica.

To heirs of John Bowling, negro Delia.

To godson Aloysius Bowling, my silver watch.

To nephew James Semmes son of Thos, ½ or moiety of the balance of my estate.

To nephews Marsham Bowling and William Queen, the other moiety or ½ part of the balance of my estate. Also 70 dollars to take care of the old negroes.

To the trustees or directors of George Town College, 37 and a half dollars.

To the Reverend Mr. Charles Neale (for the monastery) 20 dollars & to the priest the congregation 12 and a half dollars.

Item: it is expressly to be understood that all the above property of every description bequeath be retained by my sister Clementine Queen during her life for her use.

Executor: nephews Marsham Bowling and William Queen
Signed: December 8, 1817   Sarah Queen
Wit: James Boarman, Samuel Jameson

Page 5.

John Posey, Will, November 25, 1817; March 18, 1818
I, John Posey of CC, being in a low state of health, but of sound and
    disposing mind, memory and understanding;
To nephew Robert Posey, 6 pewter plates and 1 pewter dish.
To George Dunnington, the son of Francis E. Dunnington, the whole of
    my estate reserving nevertheless the use and benefit of the same
    to my sister Ann Woodward and at her death to him.
Executor: friend Francis E. Dunnington
Signed: November 25, 1817   John Posey
Wit: Thomas Price Sr., Middleton M. Rison

Page 7.

Anthony Levie, Will, February 18, 1818; March 18, 1818
I, Anthony Levie;
To wife Ann Levie, all my estate real and personal until my youngest
    living daughter arrives to the age of 16 and then my wife to take
    her thirds of the estate and the balance divided between all my
    children.
Executor: wife Ann Levie
Signed: February 18, 1818   Anthony Levie
Wit: James Naylor of George, Naylor Harbin, Roswell Harbin

Page 8.

Col. Francis Newman, Will & 2 Codicils, September 25, 1817; March
18, 1818
I, Francis Newman of CC, being weak in body, but of sound and
    disposing mind;
To sister Susan Bird Friers a room in my house with my family during
    her single life.
To wife Elizabeth Hannah Newman whose maiden name was
    Elizabeth Hannah Friers, during her single life, all my estate, real
    and personal in the USA or Great Britain and after her death or
    marriage to my children; Francis Newman, Elizabeth Rachel
    Woodyear, John Francis Newman, Francis Hollis Newman, Emily
    Newman, Susan Bird Newman and Francis Otis Newman.
Executor: wife Elizabeth Hannah Newman

Signed: September 25, 1817   Francis Newman
Wit: Nicholas Stonestreet, John Weems, Charles Sewall
Codicil 1:
To wife Elizabeth Hannah Newman, the farm on which I now live
   called "Grange" 800 acres, in trust to convey a fee simple estate
   to Wilfred Manning.
To wife Elizabeth Hannah Newman, tract of land called "Benfield"
   lying about 2 miles below Port Tobacco and is the land on which
   Francis Sewall now lives and which was purchased by me from
   the representatives of the late Doctor Daniel Jenifer containing
   1000 acres in trust to sell and dispose of the same and apply the
   purchase money first to the extinguishment of any claim in the
   US and second to satisfy all judgments against me.
Signed: September 30, 1817   F. Newman.
Wit: Nicholas Stonestreet, Mary Sewall, Ann Franklin
Codicil 2:
Imprimis: I empower wife Elizabeth H. Newman, to execute any deed
   or instrument in law conveying my right and property in and to
   lands in CC and sold to Hugh Cox and also to John A. Dyer
   according to separate contracts with them.
To sister Susan Bird Friers, 1000 dollars.
In the event of the death or marriage or refusal of my wife to stand to
   and abide to my will, I hereby appoint sister Susan Bird Friers
   and my son John Francis Newman, Executrix and Executor. And
   in the same event I hereby commit the guardianship of my infant
   children, namely, Francis Hollis Newman, Emily Newman, Susan
   Bird Newman and Francis Olis Newman unto my sister Susan
   Bird Friers during their minority.
Signed: undated   F. Newman.
Wit: Francis Digges, Charles Sewall, Catharine Sewall

Page 13.
John Baily, Will,   January 9, 1818; April 14, 1818
I, John Baily of CC, being in bad health of body, but of sound and
   disposing mind, memory and understanding;
To wife Hannah Baily, all my property during her single life and after
   her death to sons James Baily, Joseph Baily, Noah Baily, John
   Baily, Ignatius Baily, Cornelius Baily and daughter Susannah
   Baily.
Joint Executors: wife Hannah Baily and son James Baily
Signed: January 9, 1818   John Baily
Wit: Charles Lancaster, John M. T. Brooke

4

Page 15.

Mary Ann Posey, Will, March 19, 1818; April 14, 1818

I, Mary Ann Posey of CC, being sick and weak in body, but of sound and
  disposing mind, memory and understanding;

To step mother Elizabeth Posey of Charles County, 150 dollars.

To Catharine Posey daughter of Vincent Posey of Charles County, 150
  dollars.

To Clarissa Posey daughter of Vincent Posey of Charles County, my
  horse, saddle & bridle.

To Uncle Vincent Posey of Charles County, all the rest and residue of
  my estate.

Executor: Uncle Vincent Posey

Signed: March 19, 1818   Mary Ann Posey

Wit: John Herbert, Mary Bradley

Page 16.

Walter Beavin, {Beaven} Will, July 29, 1817; June 9, 1818

I, Walter Biven of CC, being of well disposed mind, will and memory;

To son Francis, negro Peter, with the stock and furniture already
  given.

To daughter Mary Calico, negro Lucy, 1 bed and furniture, 1 cow and
  calf, 1 young sorrel mare, 2 ewes and lambs, 1 sow and pigs.

Grandson William Walter Biven negro Harry after the death of my
  wife.

To son Walter, negro Gusty after the death of my wife.

To daughter Sophia, negro Allen after the death of my wife.

To son Thomas, negro Alextious after the death of my wife.

To daughter Teresa negro Catharine after the death of my wife.

To wife Charity, all the residue of my real and personal property
  during her natural life. After her death, my three daughters
  Elizabeth, Sophia and Teresa should have their single lives in my
  land after which, I devise to all my children equally in the land
  and the personal property divided amongst my four children,
  Walter, Sophia, Thomas and Teresa.

Executor: wife Charity Beaven

Signed: July 29, 1817   Walter Beavin

Wit: Thomas Lancaster, Benedict Simpson, John F. Lancaster

Page 19.

Susannah Hawkins Ware, Will, July 5, 1817; June 12, 1818

I, Susannah Hawkins Ware of CC, being in perfect health of body, and
  of sound and disposing mind, memory and understanding;

To sister Sally Maddox, wife of John Maddox, 20 dollars.

5

To brother William Ware, 20 dollars.
To niece Ann Augusta Ware, 20 dollars.
To negro Jude the annual sum of 10 dollars for and during her life.
To nieces Marion Eliza Warren Maddox and Salley Maria Maddox,
  daughters of John and Sally Maddox all the sums of money that I
  may have in possession at my death., 2 bed, bedsteads and
  furniture. Also negroes Roger (for 2 years) and Washington (for
  6 years) and then freed. If nieces should die before lawful age,
  then to nephew Robert Bruce Maddox son of John Maddox.
Executor: friend William T. Maddox
Signed: July 5, 1817   Susannah H Ware
Wit: Violetta T. Maddox, William J. Morris, Wm T. Maddox

Page 22.
Philip Thomas Marshall, Will, February 16, 1818; June 9, 1818
I, Philip T Marshall of CC, being sick and weak of body, but of sound
  and disposing mind, memory and understanding;
To wife Jane S. Marshall, the plantation whereon I now reside
  (unnamed) containing 100 acres during her single life. Also
  slaves; Sam, Gerard, Morris Henry, Henny, Mariah, Avis & Jane.
  Also my stock of horned cattle, horses, sheep and hogs,
  plantation utensils, stock of provisions laid in for present year,
  household and kitchen furniture.
To nephew John Henry Hardesty, my plantation after the death or
  marriage of my wife. Also negro James.
Executor: wife Jane S. Marshall
Signed: February 16, 1818   Philip T Marshall
Wit: Matthew W. Courtney, Gerard N. Davis, Alexander Higgs

Page 24.
John Acton Robey, Will, November 13, 1815; August 1, 1818
I, John Acton Robey of CC, being in a weak and low of health but of
  sound mind and memory;
To son John Robey, 1 horse, saddle and bridle.
To wife Eleanor Robey, all the remainder of my estate during her
  natural life and then to my children; Asseneth, Virlinder,
  Theodore, Nancy and John.
Executor: wife Eleanor Robey
Signed: November 13, 1815   John Acton Roby
Wit: Alexander Robey Sr., Elisha Robey, William Hunt

Page 26.
Mary Beavin, Will, August 12, 1815; August 20, 1818

6

I, Mary Beaven of CC, wife of John Beaven with the joint approbation of my said husband being sick and weak of body, but of sound and disposing mind, memory and understanding;

To my youngest children; Henry, James, Juliet, Elizabeth Wright, Horatio, two tracts of land called "Homsley" and "Nottingham" containing in both tracts 200 acres.

Executor: sons John Beavin, James B. Beavin

Signed: August 12, 1815   Mary Beavin

Wit: James Naylor, Charles Brandt, James Brandt, Edward Brandt

Page 28.

Philip Edelen, Will & Codicil August 19, 1818; August 24, 1818

I, Philip Edelen of CC, being sick and weak of body, but of sound and disposing mind, memory and understanding;

To brother-in-law Joseph Gardiner, all my mill lot being the same devised me by my father and my two brothers Richard and Samuel containing 80 acres in fee simple.

Item: my executors to sell the rest and residue of my land on the following terms; 1/3 cash, 1/3 in 12 months, and 1/3 in 2 years.

Item: my executors to sell all my personal estate except negro George.

To sister Dorothy Gardiner, negro George (carpenter), on condition that he shall never be sold out of her family.

To sister Arrayminta, now in the monastery, 30 pounds.

To Reverend Mr. Anger, now pastor of this congregation, 80 dollars.

To nephew Philip Gardiner, 300 dollars.

To niece Teresa Gardiner, 150 dollars.

To nephew Richard Gardiner, 150 dollars.

To brother Richard Edelen, sister Dorothy Gardiner and sister Elizabeth Simms, all the rest and residue of the proceeds of my estate.

Executor: brother-in-law Joseph Gardiner and nephew Richard Gardiner

Signed: August 19, 1818   Philip Edelen

Wit: Theodore Mudd, Thomas C. Reeves, William Queen

Codicil:

To niece Teresa Simms, 150 dollars.

Signed: August 19, 1818   Philip Edelen

Wit: Theodore Mudd, Thomas C. Reeves, William Queen

Page 31.

Jeremiah Bowling, Will, September 11, 1812; August 25, 1818

I, Jeremiah Bowling of CC a free man of colour, being at present much indisposed but of sound mind, memory and understanding;

To wife Henrietta, 1/3 part of my remaining property after debts.
The remaining 2/3 of my estate to be sold and distributed to my
children who are slaves.
Executor: Mr. Walter Beaven
Signed: September 11, 1812   Jeremiah Bowling
Wit: Thomas Lancaster, Samuel Amery

Page 33.
Somerset Posey, Will, October 15, 1815; September 14, 1818
I, Somerset Posey of CC, being sick in body, but of sound and disposing
mind, will, memory and understanding;
To wife Elizabeth Posey, all the personal & real property.
Executrix: wife Elizabeth Posey
Signed: October 15, 1815   Somerset Posey
Wit: Walbert Belaine Posey, Richard Oakley

Page 34.
Nicholas Frederick Blacklock, Will & Codicil, August 4, 1818; August
26, 1818
I, Nicholas Frederick Blacklock of the town and county of Alexandria
in the District of Columbia, being low in health, but of sound and
disposing mind, memory and understanding;
To my executors, all my estate real personal or mixed as well in
Maryland and Virginia as in the District of Columbia in trust for
the purposes hereinafter.
Item: Whereas I am engaged in commercial pursuits with my brother
Robert S. Blacklock under the firm of Nicholas and Robert
Blacklock, I direct my executors to settle my interests in said
concern, and sell and dispose of all my real estate and make
distribution of the funds which remain as follows:
To wife 1/3 of the whole and the residue to my children equally except
my horse, saddle and bridle to friend Thomas Mundell.
Executors: Thomas Mundell of Prince George's County, Maryland, and
brother-in-law William Ramsey of Alexandria, DC
Signed: August 4, 1818   N F Blacklock
Wit: Clement Dorsey, Robert Mandelville, J.H.H. Penn
Codicil: I give my watch that I wear to son Nicholas Frederick
Blacklock and my gold repeating watch to my daughter Jane.
Signed: August 4, 1818   N F Blacklock
Wit: Clement Dorsey, Robert Mandelville, J.H.H. Penn
Charles County Sct. August 26, 1818; then came Thomas Mundell one
of the executors of Nicholas F Blacklock late of Charles County,
deceased.

Page 36.
Stephen Latimer Jr., Will, August 17, 1815; September 19, 1818
I, Stephen Latimer Jr., of CC, being in perfect health mind and memory;
To relation Joseph King, 1 horse, saddle and bridle, value of 150
dollars and 500 dollars cash also a home on my possession I now
owneth so long as he may think proper.
To servant Juliet, a mulatter girl shall be free at 21 yrs.
To wife Hannah Elizabeth all my land I now possess with all my
personal estate during her life and after to be equally divided
between my three daughters, Ann Elizabeth, Louisa and Sarah
Rebekah.
Executrix: wife Hannah Elizabeth Latimer
Signed: August 17, 1815   Stephen Latimer Jr.
Oath that will was in deceased handwriting: Aquila Bateman, John M.
Brown

Page 38.
Walter Bond, Will, March 9, 1818; October 1, 1818
I, Walter Bond of CC, Tho weak of body, yet of sound and perfect
memory and understanding;
To wife Ann Bond, the whole of my property real and personal for the
benefit of herself and children during single life and if she
remarries, then she shall have nothing but what is to come from
her fathers estate.
Item: If my son John Bond should be ungovernable and will not be
dutiful to his mother, then he should be bound to some good
mechanic till he is 21 yrs. and 6 to 12 months schooling.
Executor: wife Ann Bond
Signed: March 9, 1818   Walter Bond
Wit: Wilson Compton, James B. Latimer, Charles Turner

Page 39.
Elizabeth Harris, Will, July 28, 1817; October 29, 1818
I, Elizabeth Harris of Pickawaxen in CC, being perfect health of body,
and of sound and disposing mind, memory and understanding;
To sister Violetta Harris all my estate both real and personal.
Item I direct that there shall be no inventory returned of my said
estate to the orphans court.
Executrix: sister Violetta Harris
Signed: July 28, 1817   Elizabeth Harris
Wit: Ann Gwinn Vincent, William Courts, Thomas H. Maddox

Page 41.

Mary Noble Stonestreet, Will, September 3, 1818; December 7, 1818

I, Mary N. Stonestreet of CC, being sick and weak in body, but of sound and disposing mind, memory and understanding;

To daughter Jane Digges, {negroes} Betty Day, Basil and Mary's child Celistia, Caroline.

To grandson, Francis Neale, negro James.

To granddaughter Mary Eleanor Neale, negroes Eliza and her child William, and 1 bed and furniture.

To granddaughter Catharine Neale, negro Halena.

To son Joseph Noble Stonestreet, negro Bob and his wife Henny and their children Eleanor and John, Henry Day, and Walter Dodson and 1 bed and furniture and whatever may appear to be due me from Doctor James Edelen's estate.

To granddaughter Mary E. Stonestreet, girl Maria.

To son Nicholas Stonestreet, boy William.

To grandson Charles Henry Stonestreet, negro Richard.

To grandson Nicholas Stonestreet Jr., negro Charles Grandison.

To son Henry Stonestreet, negro John, 1 bed and furniture.

To sons Joseph Noble Stonestreet and Nicholas Stonestreet, jointly negroes Frederick, Harry and Mary. 1 bed and furniture, 1 large dining table, 6 leather chairs, 1 cart and yoke of oxen, table and teaspoons, china and the balance of my furniture.

To son Lewis Stonestreet, if ever he should marry and have lawful issue then the last devise to sons Joseph Noble Stonestreet and Nicholas Stonestreet to be given to the issue of son Lewis.

Executor: none named

Signed: September 3, 1818   Mary N. Stonestreet

Wit: Edward J. Heard, Mary Jones

Page 43.

William Mason, Will & Codicil, October 7, 1817; December 8, 1818

I, William Mason of CC, being of perfect and sound mind and memory and in good health

To wife Ann Mason, for and during the term of her natural life, 500 dollars per annum to be paid by all my five children or my executor out of the property of such of them as shall not have arrived at the age of 21 yrs or married in the following proportions to wit: each of my three sons shall pay ¼ part and each of my two daughters 1/8th part on the first day of January, but if my wife shall not agree and stand to this will but claim her thirds then my eldest son shall pay their 1/4th parts to my three youngest children.

To wife Ann Mason, the use of 10 negroes, ½ male ½ female and after her death to my 5 children.

To wife Ann Mason, my carriage and horses and all my household and kitchen furniture and all the plate and at her death to my two daughters if unmarried.

To wife Ann Mason, use of ¼ of my stock of horses, cows, sheep and hogs and at her death to my 3 youngest children.

To eldest son William Mason, the following 12 negroes; Toney, Guss, Louis, Abram, Lucy, Nely, Eleanor, Leannah, Mathelda, Joshua and Henny all in his possession.

To second son George Mason, the following 13 negroes; George, Harry, John, Henry, Peter, Anne, Mary, Hannah, Liza, Cintha, Lilly, Ozz and Franny the daughter of Hannah all in his possession.

To third son Edgar Eilbeck Mason and my two daughters Ann Sarah Stuart Mason and Mary Elizabeth Mason at the age of 21 yrs or marriage, each of them four negro men, two boys, three women and three girls.

To wife Ann Mason, 70 barrels of corn and three of flour per annum paid by my children or my executors in the aforementioned proportions.

Item: I direct that all the land I die possessed of in Maryland at my decease to be sold by my executors for the benefit and support of my three youngest children until they are of age or marry and money arising divided as follows: ½ to be laid out in bank stock or such landed property to be the property of my 3rd son Edgar Eilbeck Mason at 21 yrs, 1/3 of remainder to be laid out in landed property and houses as a home of residence for my wife and daughters and to remain the property of my wife for and during her natural life and then to my two daughters during their single lives and then sold; the remaining 2/3 (of the ½) to be laid out in bank stock or such landed property to be the property of my two daughters at 21 yrs or marriage.

To wife Ann Mason, during her natural life, my dwelling house and all the out houses on the lot adjacent with my garden and orchards to be considered as a home and residence for my two daughters during their single lives.

Item: I direct that the remainder of my lands be cultivated or rented out for the benefit and support of my three youngest children until they are of age or marry then divided as follows; ½ to third son Edgar Eilbeck Mason and the other half between my two daughters Ann Sarah Stuart and Mary Elizabeth Mason.

Item: I direct that all my lands in Kentucky to be sold and 1/6 part of the money arising to my wife and the balance to my 5 children at age or marriage.

Executors: two eldest sons William Mason and George Mason, and two friends Richard Stuart and Townshend S. Dade both of King George County, Virginia (guardians)

Signed: October 7, 1817   Wm Mason

Wit: Joseph N. Stonestreet, William Brawner, James N. Hickey {did not appear at probate}, George Jenkins, James B. Pye

Codicil: as there are several debts owing to me from different persons and particularly from my brother John Mason as partner of the House of Fenwick Mason & Company on account of shipments made them during his residence in France, also my part of a considerable sum of money due from said House to the representatives of the late Col George Mason do direct that all monies recovered and the money arising from the sale of a small tract of land in the neighborhood of Port Tobacco, shall be first appropriated to paying a debt now owing from me to George F. Thornton of King George County, Virginia and the residue to my three youngest children.

Signed: January 9, 1818   Wm Mason.

Charles County Sct; December 8th 1818, then came George Mason (of Gunston Virginia) and made oath that he was familiar with the hand writing of William Mason deceased.

Page 51.

Catharine T. Meek, Will,   October 31, 1818; December 7, 1818

I, Catharine T. Meek of CC, being weak in body yet in perfect mind and memory;

To my five daughters; Catharine Ann Ireland Semms, Harriot Simms, Elizabeth Ward Adams, Taliaferro Hooe Smith, Mary Ann Dent Ireland Middleton, all my personal and real property.

Executor: William H. Winter of Mississippi Territory

Signed: October 31, 1818   Catharine T. Meek

Wit: John Perry, Sylvester Skinner, Sarah B. Posey

Page 52.

John Adler Clements, Will,   September 27, 1818; January 4, 1819

I, John Adler Clements of CC, being sick and weak of body, but of sound and disposing mind, memory and understanding;

To wife Eleanor Clements, the whole of my property during her natural life and at her decease to be devised in what manner she may think proper.

Executor: wife Eleanor Clements

Signed: September 27, 1818   John Adler Clements

Wit: Gustavus A. Adams, David Simmons, Joseph Simmes

Page 54.

Thomas Monroe Sr., Will, 26 January 1815; January 5, 1819

I, Thomas Monroe of CC, being weak of body, but of sound disposing mind and memory;

To nephew Thomas Monroe, negro Judd, 1 gray mare and all my plantation utensils.

To Ann Monroe daughter of Thomas Monroe, negro Joe.

To Mary Monroe daughter of Thomas Monroe, 1 bed and furniture, and 1 young cow.

To Mary Cox daughter of Charles Cox, 1 young cow.

To John Cox, 1 grey horse.

To George Downs, 1 cow.

To Rebecca Cox, 1 bed and furniture, 1 punch bowl, 1 pitcher, 1 decanter, 1 pepper caster and 1 sugar bowl.

To Sophia Monroe, 40 dollars.

To Sarah Monroe, 20 dollars.

Executor: nephew Thomas Monroe

Signed: 26 January 1815   Thomas Monroe

Wit: William A. Griffin, Henry Brawner Jr.

Page 56.

Thomas I{saac} Reeves, Will, June 18, 1818; January 25, 1819

I, Thomas I. Reeves of CC, being in perfect mind and memory; and to be buried in the Episcopal faith

To Rebecca H. Reeves, negro Ann, 1 bed and furniture, 1 cow and calf, 1 mare, bridle and saddle.

To Hezekiah J. Reeves, negro Pries, and 60 dollars.

To second daughter Mary E. Huntt, negro Fielder.

To Thomas W. Reeves, negro Lucinder, 1 bed and furniture, 1 desk & looking glass, 1 horse, saddle and bridle.

To daughter Permealy Reeves, negro Prucilla, 1 bed and furniture, 1 cow and calf, 1 horse, saddle and bridle.

To Charles F. Reeves, negro Charity, 1 bed and furniture, 1 cow and calf, 50 dollars.

To Josiah W. Reeves, negro Susannah, 1 bed and furniture, 1 cow and calf, ½ dozen flag bottom chairs, 1 razor and shaving box and razor case, 1 cabinet box, 1 looking glass with all my wearing apparel.

Item: in case I should marry a second wife, it is my will that she should have her just part of my whole estate real and personal during her natural life, and then divided amongst my and her children.

Executor: Thomas W. Reeves and Doctor James Reeves
Signed: June 18, 1818   Thomas I. Reeves
Wit: Wilson Smoot, Hezekiah W. Robinson, Henry W. Hardy
Linda Reno note: Mary Hunt d/o Thomas Isaac Reeves was married to
Judson Hunt.

Page 58.

Benjamin Davis, Will,   October 14, 1816; March 10, 1819
I, Benjamin Davis of CC, being sick and weak in body, but of sound and
    disposing mind, memory and understanding;
To two eldest daughters Mary Cawood Harrison and Elizabeth Thorn
    Lyon, the property they were given at their marriage, viz;
    negroes, stock, and furniture, and appraised with my other
    personal property.
To four youngest daughters, Sarah T. Davis, Cecelia A. Davis, Jane C.
    Davis and Lucinda Davis the same amount in negroes, stock and
    furniture to make equal with my two eldest daughters.
Executor: Sarah Davis
Signed: October 14, 1816   Benjamin Davis
Wit: George Dyson, William Thorn, George Davis

Page 60.

Eleanor Dent, Will,   November 14, 1818; March 24, 1819
I, Eleanor Dent of CC, being at present in a low and sickly state of
    health but of a sound and disposing mind, memory and
    understanding;
To niece Elizabeth Dent Peyton, 1/6 part of the appraisement amount
    of my slaves.
To nephew Johannis Greenfield Dent Storke, 1/6 part of the
    appraisment amount of my slaves.
To sister Jane Dent the residue of my personal estate and whereas it
    is my wish that the children of my brothers and sister Ann
    Parnham should (after the death of my sister Jane, to whom from
    a sense of obligation and gratitude I now leave the greater part
    of my estate) receive a part of my negro property, I therefore
    request her to secure by will or otherwise to the children of my
    brothers Henry Dent and George Dent and of my sister Ann
    Parnham a portion of the negro property.
Executor: sister Jane Dent
Signed: November 14, 1818   Eleanor Dent
Wit: George Brent, Horatio C. McElderry, Joseph Lancaster

14

Page 62.

Margaret Ann Mudd, Will,   February 4, 1816; March 26, 1819

I, Margaret Ann Mudd of CC, being sick and weak of body, but of sound
and disposing mind, memory and understanding;

To granddaughter Margaret Montgomery, 1 spotted heifer, 1 bed and
furniture, 1 bay mare.

To son Walter Mudd, negro Jim, and to pay ½ the annual value or hire
of said negro Jim to granddaughter Margaret Montgomery
during her single life.

To daughter Sary Mudd, negro Mary.

To son Walter Mudd, my falltop desk.

To grandson William Mudd, all the rest and residue of my estate.

Executor: son Walter Mudd

Signed: February 4, 1816   Margaret Ann Mudd

Wit: Theodore Mudd, John W. Wright

Page 64.

Richard B. Meek, Will,   February 15, 1815; April 2, 1819

I, Richard B. Meek of CC, being in perfect health of body mind and
memory;

To wife Catharine T{aliaferro} Meek the use of the lands devised to me
by my father during her natural life and then to my brother
Joseph H. Meek, and after his death to nephew Richard B. Posey,
son of James Posey, but if he should die in his minority, then
equally divided between his surviving sisters.

To Mary Ann Dent Ireland Middleton, a bay colt.

Executor: wife Catharine T. Meek

Signed: February 15, 1815   Richard B. Meek

Wit: Francis R. Speake, William Winter Dunnington, Taliaferro Hooe
Middleton

Charles County Sct. April 2nd 1819, then came R{ichard} T{hompson}
Semmes and made oath. {mm note: wife Catharine T. Meek {nee
Hooe} had died and her will was probated December 7, 1818,
refer to page 51 of this will book}

Page 66.

Walbert Belaine Posey, Will,   June 11, 1818; May 21, 1819

I, Walbert Belaine Posey of CC, being sick in body, but strong judgment
reason and understanding;

Item: my property to be equally divided between my daughter Sarah
Julia Posey and her mother Sarah E. Posey.

Item: the 2/3 of the property belonging to my daughter Sarah Julia
Posey to be placed in the hands of Capt. Laurence Posey and John

M. Posey and taken under their care and protection, educated until capable of going to the female academy (George Town College) where I wish her to go.

To brother John M. Posey, all my clothing, double barrel gun, and fishing tackle and boat that I bought of Laurence Posey together with her rigging colors, and the oldest clothing he will give to my servant Davy.

Executor: brothers Capt. Laurence Posey and John M. Posey
Signed: June 11, 1818   W.B. Posey
Wit: Elizabeth Posey, Allen Sweny

Page 67.
Alexander Jones McConchie, Will, April 21, 1819; May 26, 1819
I, Alexander Jones McConchie of CC, being sick and weak of body, but of sound and disposing mind, memory and understanding;

Imprimis, negro woman Levina and her four children, Louisa, Chloe Ann, William Henry and Mary (not christened yet) to be emancipated and discharged from slavery. I also discharge from slavery, my negro woman Linney and her two children Richard Carroll and Salley.

To negro woman Levina and her four children above named, the following parcel of land, beginning at the head of valley where the main road leading from Port Tobacco to the Hill Top forks to go to Cedar Point Neck until it intersects a tract of land called "Lindsay", all the land on the west side. Also 1 feather bed and furniture, 1 cow and calf, 1 black horse, the use of my kitchen until there can be a house built.

To brother Thomas McConchie all the rest and residue of my estate real or personal, provided he will build a house on the land bequeathed to Levina and her children and covered with short shingles and to have a brick fireplace.

Executor: brother Thomas McConchie
Signed: April 21, 1819   Alexr J.McConchie
Wit: John Meredith, Gerard Robertson, John Edelen

Page 70.
Michael Gardiner, Will, February 4, 1819; June 8, 1819
I, Michael Gardiner of CC, being weak and sick of body, but of sound and disposing mind, memory and understanding;

Item, it is my will that my female slave Hetty, purchased of Leonard Mudd, shall be free at the age of 16 yrs.

Executor: father William Gardiner
Signed: February 4, 1819   Michael Gardiner

16

Wit: Leonard Mudd, Thomas D. Perrie

Page 72.
Catharine Walker, Will & Codicil, January 19, 1818; June 21, 1819
I, Catharine Walker of CC, being weak and low of body, but of sound
and disposing mind, memory and understanding;
To son Thomas Hawkins, negroes; London, Grandison, Sarah, and
Mary, all my stock of horses, ½ my stock of cattle, ½ stock of
sheep, all my stock of hogs, ½ my household and kitchen
furniture, all my fowls, 2 small stills, 1 yoke of steers and cart,
and all my plantation utensils. Also 1 large looking glass now
standing in my hall.
To my 5 granddaughters and grandson, the children of my daughter
Jane Jameson, 30 dollars each.
To my grandsons and granddaughters, the children of my son
Alexander Smith Henley Hawkins and my daughter Elizabeth
Hanson to each and equal proportion of what may remain.
Executor: friend Joseph A. Turner
Signed: January 19, 1818   Catharine Walker
Wit: Sarah Waters, Elkanah Waters, Joseph Harrison
Codicil: To my grandchildren now living in Kentucky, children of my
son Alexander Smith Henley Hawkins and my daughter Elizabeth
Hanson, the following negroes; Edward, Mary, Catharine,
Leonard, Polly, Eleanor and Smith, after the death of my child
Henry Smith Hawkins.
Signed: February 6, 1818   Catharine Walker
Wit: Elkanah Waters, Elizabeth Waters, Joseph A. Turner

Page 76.
William Cooke Sr., Will, April 26, 1819; July 6, 1819
I, William Cooke of CC, being weak and infirm, but of well recollected
mind;
To son William Cooke, tract "Littlewood Forest" 100 acres, but now
known by the name "Twins", it being the plantation he now
dwells. Also negroes; James and George.
To daughter Mary Mudd, negroes Peter, Terry and Rachel.
To son Richard Cooke, part of tract "Littlewood Forest" 100 acres, and
now called "Twins", it being the plantation he now dwells.
To daughter Mary Hagan, negroes Elisha, Peg, Celia and Jerry.
To daughter Sarah Beavin, negroes, Anny, John, Dorothy and Delia.
To grandson William Henry Cooke, negro Raphael.
To Reverend Robert Angier, 20 dollars for masses for myself and my
friends who have gone before me.

To Mary Mudd, 20 dollars.

To son William Cooke, old negroes Jim and Nan to be my him taken care of and in consideration will receive 100 dollars extra.

Item: son Richard Cooke put in the 147 dollars I loaned him in the residue of my estate equally divided.

Item: Walter Mudd put in the 50 dollars I loaned him in the residue of my estate equally divided.

Executor: son William Cooke

Signed: April 26, 1819   William Cooke Sr.

Wit: James Reeves, Edward Jenkins, William Fletcher

Page 78.

Richard B. Clements, Will, April 15, 1819; July 6, 1819

I, being now weak and very infirm;

To wife Martha Clements, negroes Catherine, Eleanor, Rebecah and Samuel, all my stock, household and kitchen furniture.

To Raphael Wheatley, negroes George Henry reserving the use of him for my wife and Sandy the property of Catharine Wheatley dec'd.

Executors: wife Martha Clements and Raphael Wheatley

Signed: April 15, 1819   Richard B. Clements

Wit: James Reeves, Thomas Padgett, Margaret A. Montgomery

Page 80.

Benjamin Padgett, Will, June 5, 1819; August 21, 1819

I, Benjamin Padgett being sick and weak, but having a right disposing mind and memory;

To two daughters Mary Padgett and Sarah Padgett, each a feather bed and furniture.

To wife Elizabeth Padgett all the remaining part of my property real personal and mixed during her lifetime and after her decease to my children.

Executor: none nominated

Signed: June 5, 1819   Benjamin Padgett

Wit: Edward D. Arvin, Henry Padgett, Edward Arvin

Charles County Sct. August 21st 1819, then came Hezekiah Padgett son of Benjamin Padgett and made oath the will was that of the testator.

Page 81.

Robert Bruce, Will, August 14, 1819; September 2, 1819

I, Robert Bruce of CC, being sick and weak of body, but of sound and disposing mind, memory and understanding;

To nephew Walter Bruce, negroes Dick and Harry.

To niece Jane Bruce, my sorrel mare and 15 dollars.

To John Matthews all pensions which may be due me from the USA upon the conditions that he pay unto my two nieces, Jane and Sary Bruce, each the sum of 15 dollars.

To brother William Bruce, all the residue of my estate.

Executor: brother William Bruce

Signed: August 14, 1819   Robert Bruce

Wit: John Edelen, John C. Layman

Page 82.

Walter Scroggin, Will,   December 14, 1816; September 27, 1819

I, Walter Scroggin of CC, enjoying my usual health of body and of sound and disposing mind, memory and understanding;

To friend and sister Jane Scroggin, all my estate, real, personal and mixed.

Executor: sister Jane Scroggin

Signed: December 14, 1816   Walter Scroggin

Wit: Alexander Matthews, John Edelen, William Thompson

Page 83.

Samuel Griffin, Will,   December 5, 1818; November 2, 1819

I, Samuel Griffin of CC, being in perfect health;

To wife Mary Griffin the residue of my estate after debts to dispose of as she think proper.

Executrix: wife Mary Griffin

Signed: December 5, 1818   Samuel Griffin

Wit: Charles Jones Bruce, James Owen

Page 84.

Robert Charles Jones, Will (copy),   October 11, 1819; October 26, 1819

I, Robert Charles Jones of CC, being sick and weak in body, but of sound and disposing mind, memory and understanding;

To mother Dorothy H. Storer, all my lands lying on the river Potomac containing 400 acres during her natural life and then to my brother John Courts Jones in fee simple.

To brother John Courts Jones, bonds, promissory notes and all and everything due and owing to me, to my brother upon his arrival at the age of 21 years.

Item: I bequeath a mourning ring of 10 dollars value be presented to Peter Cullin of Washington City, District of Columbia.

Executor: Richard M. Scott of Alexandria and Alexandria County, District of Columbia

Signed: October 11, 1819   Robert C. Jones
Wit: David Euston, Ebeneazer Stout, Daniel P. Porter
Certified that the aforegoing will is truly taken from the original will
    filed in the office of the Register of Wills for Washington County,
    District of Columbia this 27th day of October 1819; Henry C.
    Neale, Regr of Wills

Page 86.

Luke Wheeler, Will, May 13, 1818; October 26, 1819

I, Luke Wheeler of CC, being sick and weak of body, but of sound and
    disposing mind, memory and understanding;

To wife Ann Wheeler, all the land of which I am possessed during her
    single life, with the exception of "Planters Delight" which
    originally belonged to my uncle Clement Wheeler, and it is my
    desire that it should belong to my son William Wheeler when he
    arrives at the age of 21 yrs.

To two daughters Mary Wheeler and Henrietta Wheeler the use of the
    land in conjunction with their mother during their single lives
    and then to my son William Wheeler.

To wife Ann Wheeler, negroes; David, Oswald, Harry, Harriot, Henny
    and Betty.

To daughter Mary Wheeler, negroes; Gerrard, Peter,Teresa, Monica
    and Basil.

To son William Wheeler, negroes; John (carpenter) , Bill, Eliza and
    Milly.

To daughter Henrietta Wheeler, negroes; Charles, John, Catharine,
    Thesa and Charity.

Executors: Charles Bennett and wife Ann Wheeler
Signed: May 13, 1818   Luke Wheeler
Wit: Walter M. Millar, Philip T. Briscoe, Edward Welch

Page 88.

Lydia Dyson, Will, July 12, 1819; December 14, 1819

I, Lydia Dyson of CC, enjoying my usual reason and understanding;

To brother George Dyson, during his life, all my negro property, vizt;
    Lewis, Richard, John, Benjamin, Charles, Littleton, Elizabeth,
    Mary, Jane, Elizabeth and Martha, and after his death to his
    children.

To Henry Dyson and Ann Dyson, children of brother George Dyson, all
    the rest and residue of my estate.

Executor: brother George Dyson
Signed: July 12, 1819   Lydia Dyson
Wit: Alexander Dent, Nathan S. Dent

Page 89.

Thomas Bond, Will, July 14, 1819; December 14, 1819

I, Thomas Bond of CC, being sick and weak of body, but of sound and disposing mind, memory and understanding;

To Zachariah Bond, my youngest son, my plantation whereon I now dwell containing by patent 180 acres in fee simple.

To son Benjamin Bond, 1 feather bed and furniture.

To son Zachariah Bond, the rest and residue of my estate both real and personal.

Executor: son Zachariah Bond

Signed: July 14, 1819   Thomas Bond

Wit: Philip King, Hanson Higgs, Samuel Higgs

Page 91.

Elizabeth Smith, Will,   November 30, 1819; December 22, 1819

I, Elizabeth Smith of CC, being very sick and weak in body, but of sound and disposing mind, memory and understanding;

To daughter Elizabeth Gardiner, wife of Ignatius W. Gardiner, the following property, viz; negroes; Linder, Judah, Sarah, Henry & George sons of Judah, 1 bed and furniture which I lieth on and 1 cow and calf. Also 1 spice mortar, big turine sets in the buffet in the hall, and 6 sliver table spoons.

To three granddaughters, Harriot Cook, Louisa Smith and Catharine Smith, negro John.

To granddaughter Louisa Smith 1 bed and furniture

To granddaughter Catharine Smith, 1 desk in the hall and 1 trunk in the room.

To son Alexius Smith my white horse and use of the above property devised to granddaughters during his life.

To Reverend Mr. Robert Anger, 5 dollars for prayers for me.

Executor: George Gardiner

Signed: November 30, 1819   Elizabeth Smith

Wit: John W. McPherson, Levin Smith

Page 93.

James Montgomery, Will,   April 1, 1814; February 19, 1820

I, James Montgomery of CC, being sick, but perfectly in my senses and of sound judgment;

To wife Elizabeth Montgomery, my whole estate real and personal

Executor: none named

Signed: April 1, 1814   James Montgomery

Wit: Joshua Montgomery, James Reeves, Francis Green

Page 94.
Eleanor Hall, Will, June 2, 1816; March 4, 1820
I, Eleanor Hall of CC, being sick and weak of body, but of sound and
    disposing mind and memory;
To daughter Elizabeth Grace Hall, negroes; Daphne, Harriet and
    George, with all my stock, household furniture, plantation
    utensils and crop of every description except for the following:
To son William Nottingham, 1 yoke of oxen, and 1 young colt.
To son Wilfred Nottingham, negroes; Clare and Anthony provided he
    bring no claim against me or my estate. If he does, negroes to be
    sold to discharge debts and balance to son.
To granddaughter (unnamed), daughter of Charles Cheseldine and
    Mary his wife, negroes; Nelly and Charlotte.
Executor: daughter Elizabeth Grace Hall {Elizabeth G. Edelen at
    probate}
Signed: June 2, 1816   Eleanor Hall
Wit: John B. Edelen, John Upgate Cook

Page 95.
Elizabeth Sewall, Will, August 11, 1819; March 30, 1820
I, Elizabeth Sewall wife of Charles Sewall of CC, being at this time in a
    sick and weak situation, but of perfectly sound and disposing
    mind, memory and understanding;
Whereas by a deed of Indenture dated June 15, 1811 between Charles
    Sewall and Elizabeth Sewall his wife on one part and Francis
    Newman of the other part in consideration of 10 dollars did
    grant sundry tracts of and expressly convented and agreed that
    Francis Newman shall after the death of Elizabeth Sewall convey
    all the tracts and articles of personal property as she directs.
    Now, pursuant to the said indenture, Francis Newman shall
    convey and deliver unto my daughter Mary Goodrick Sewall, one
    moiety or half part and the other one moiety or half part to my
    daughter Sarah Matilda Sewall during her natural life, provided
    when called on to transfer to my daughter Mary Goodrick Sewall
    1/3 part in value of all the negroes which were devised by Mary
    Goodrick deceased to my children and to my son Charles Sewall,
    one other third part .
Executor: friend and kinsman Francis Sewall and daughter Mary
    Goodrick Sewall
Signed: August 11, 1819   Elizabeth Sewall
Wit: Dorothy Manning, Wilfred Manning, Muncaster Moredock

22

Page 99.

John Smith, Will, February 10, 1817; April 12, 1820

I, John Smith of CC, being sick and weak of body, but of sound mind
and memory and disposing judgment;

To wife Martha Smith, the plantation I now dwell, part of tract "The
Forrest", also tracts "Smith's Gore", and "Smiths Level" during
her life and then to John S. Davis son of George S. Davis. Also
tracts "Wiltshire" 50 acres, and "Juxta Stadium Aurectum" 90
acres, during her life and then to Caroline Davis and Mary Davis
daughters of Zacheus Davis.

To wife Martha Smith, negroes' Jeremiah, Peter, Augustin, Sarah, Clair,
Rachel, Sarah (child) , also negro Francis Xaverius and after her
death said negro to Reverend Robert Anger or whatever priest
attends the upper Zachiah congregation and 30 dollars.

To sister Jane Summers five children, negroes; Susanna, Elizabeth,
John, Henritta, Jeremiah and 200 dollars.

To John T. Clements four children named Harriot, Priscilla, Teresa and
George Washington, part of tract "The Forrest" and negro
Lurainer.

To godson Samuel Beavin, negro Joseph.

To godson James Madison Burch, negro James.

Executrix: wife Martha Smith

Signed: February 10, 1817   John Smith

Wit: John W. Wright, Daniel Townshend, Joseph Wright Jr.

mm note: tract "Juxta Stadium Aurectum" was patented by Thomas
Greenfield in 1713 and lies in Prince George's County.

Page 101.

James Fowke, Will, July 19, 1819; April 20, 1820

I, James Fowke of CC, being sick and weak of body, but of sound and
disposing mind and memory understanding;

To son William Smith Fowke, all my property real and personal after
debts.

Executor: friend George Robertson

Signed: July 19, 1819   James Fowke

Wit: William S. Jones, William W. Dunnington, George K. Milstead

Page 102.

Ignatius Wood, Will, not dated; May 1, 1820

I, Ignatius Wood of CC, being in perfect health of body and of sound
and disposing mind, memory and understanding;

To wife Ann Wood, the use of all my estate during her natural life. (the
reason of making this devise to my wife is from her unusual

industry and fidelity towards me through which a great part of my estate have been accumulated and further to prevent the disregard of our coheirs.)

To granddaughter Ann Margaret Sanders, negro Charlotta, the profits of her labor applied to education and then hers at 16 yrs or marriage.

To daughter Sarah Elizabeth S. Saunders when she was married to John F.R. Sanders, the property I gave her and the negro Charlotta which I have devised to my granddaughter Ann Margaret Sanders.

To each of my four sons, Ferdinand, William, George and Giles, a horse and saddle worth 55 dollars which will make them equal with my son Henry.

Item: after the death of my wife, all the rest and residue of my estate divided amongst my 6 sons; Henry S. Wood, Ferdinand F. Wood, William S. Wood, George L{eslie} Wood and Giles C. Wood.

Joint Executors: wife Ann Wood and William A. Tiar/Tyer
Signed: not dated   Igns Wood
Charles County Sct., May 1, 1820; Then came Thomas Burgess and John B. Edelen and made oath the will was that of the testator.

Page 104.
Edward Welch, Will, July 20, 1819; June 8, 1820
I, Edward Welch of CC, being in perfect health of body and of sound and disposing mind, memory and understanding;

To wife Teresa Welch, the use of the whole of my property during her natural or single life except as devised as follows:

To son William Welch, my young gray mare, my ox cart and 1 yoke of steers.

To son Richard Welch 1 feather bead.

To grandson Benjamin Welch son of Ann Welch, my horse colt and 1 feather bed.

Item: after the death or marriage of my wife, the whole of my estate to my children; Joseph Welch, William Welch, Edward Welch, Richard Welch, Ann Welch, Eleanor Welch and daughter Mary Clements Welch. If daughter Mary Clements Welch should die without issue, then her part to fall to the rest equally. Son Edward Welch to have management of the division.

Executors: wife Teresa Welch and son Edward Welch
Signed: July 20, 1819   Edward Welch
Wit: Gustavus A. Adams, Richard R. Swann, William Garner

24

Page 106.

Ann Davis, Nucuputive {Oral} Will, May 19 1820; June 14, 1820

The last will and testament of Ann Davis, late of CC, deceased by word of mouth when sick of the sickness whereof she died in the presence of us the subscribers; May 19 1820, John Delozier Sr, Ann Wheeler.

Item: it was her wish that her 2 cows and 1 calf, 1 cupboard and 1 chest should be given to John Delozier Jr.

Item: that the residue of her property except one chintz frock should be given to Phebe Welch and the chintz frock should be given to Mary Ann Delozier eldest daughter of Richard Delozier.

Charles County Sct., June 14, 1820; then came John Delozier Sr. and Ann Wheeler and made oath the above words were those spoken by the said Ann Davis.

Page 106.

Sarah Keech, Nucuputive {Oral} Will, July 7, 1819; July 10, 1819

The last will and testament of Sarah Keech late of CC deceased declared by word of mouth July 7, 1819 when sick with the sickness whereof she died, in the presence of the subscribers, that all she left should be given to Olivia Turner daughter of Ann K. Turner. In witness we have hereto have set our hands this July 10, 1819.

Wit: Sarah Turner, Ann K. Turner, Eliza Turner, Joseph T. Turner

Page 107.

Rose Matthews, Will, June 4, 1819; July 17, 1820

I, Rose Matthews of CC, being sick and weak of body, but of sound and disposing mind, memory and understanding;

To son-in-law William D{uhurst} Merrick, negroes; Frederick, Daniel and Rose in use and upon trust to aid in the education of my four youngest sons, Francis Matthews, Charles Henry Matthews, William Matthews and Thomas Matthews, and it is my will that he should sell said negroes and I hope that this money together with the income of other property will prove sufficient to give each of them college education.

To servant maids, Charity, Lucy and Anny, each 20 dollars in consideration of their long and faithful services.

To Susan Oliver 20 dollars in consideration of her faithful services.

Executor: son-in-law William D. Merrick

Signed: June 4, 1819   Rose Matthews

Wit: John H. Weems, E.A. Middleton, E. C. Lucas

Page 109.
Prior Berry, Will, April 28, 1820; July 21, 1820
It is the will of God to place me in a weak state and being in perfect
    senses and for the benefit of my beloved wife;
To daughter Permelia Marlow, John Berry, Mary E. Gates, Meaky A.
    Giddens, Nathaniel Berry, Thomas Humphrey Berry the sum of
    twenty five cents.
To son Thomas Smallwood Berry all the property I die possessed of,
    and that my wife should have use of it during her life.
Executor: son Thomas Smallwood Berry (last married son)
Signed: April 28, 1820   Prior Berry
Wit: Sylvester F. Gardiner, Ignatius Gardiner

Page 110.
Matilda Nalley, Will,   December 17, 1819; August 16, 1820
I, Matilda Nalley of CC, of low state of health, but of perfect mind and
    disposing memory;
To brother John Nalley, 100 dollars.
To brother-in-law Benjamin Simpson, the whole entire balance of my
    property authorizing him to receive and settle my estate.
Executor: Benjamin Simpson {called Benedict Simpson at probate}
Signed: December 17, 1819   Matilda Nalley
Wit: William Corry, Edward Edelen Sr.

Page 111.
Benjamin Beavin, Will,   June 24, 1820; November 9, 1820
I, Benjamin Beavin of CC, being very sick and weak in body, but of
    perfect mind and memory;
To son Charles Beavin, the tract of land where I now live "Huckleberry
    Swamp" and "Hickory Thicket".
To daughter Elizabeth Mary Beavin, the use of "Hickory Thicket"
    during her single life.
To four children; Susannah Richards, James Hoye Beavin, Elizabeth
    Mary Beavin and Charles Beavin all my negroes except James
    whom I have given to daughter Elizabeth Mary Beavin
    heretofore. Negroes vizt; Ann, Molbro, Powell, Benjamin,
    Calister, Ann (small) , Samuel, Eliza, Jane, John, Alexander,
    Charity, Harriet, Rucka.
To granddaughter Cassandra Richards, negro Jane.
To four children aforesaid, all my stock of horses, cattle, sheep, hogs,
    household and kitchen furniture and plantation utensils equally.
Executors: daughter Elizabeth Mary Beavin and son Charles Beavin
Signed: June 24, 1820   Benjamin Beavin

Wit: William Turner Jr., Theodore Mudd, Henry H. Bean

Page 113.

Kitty Sewall, Will, not dated; September 1, 1820

I, Kitty Sewall of CC, being of sound and disposing mind, memory and understanding but low in body and health;

To Levin Watson, in as much as I have no personal property of any value I bequeath and devise all the real estate of what I am possessed to him in trust for him to sell and as I am indebted to him in consideration of debts paid by him for me, or for which he is now legally responsible for board and other necessaries furnished by him, it is my will that the money arising from the sale of my land should satisfy his claim as ascertained and settled by the orphans court.

To my half brother William Wiseman, the residue of the monies arising from the sale of my lands after debts paid at 21 yrs subject to the discretion of the orphans court.

Executor: Levin Watson

Signed: not dated   Kitty Sewall

Wit: Henry Brawner, Alexander Sangster, William Acton

Page 115.

Isidore Sansberrie, Will, August 24, 1820; September, 18, 1820

I, Isadore Sansberrie of CC, being sick and weak of body, but of sound and disposing mind, memory and understanding;

To sister Terecy Gwynn, all the silver plate that I possess and 100 dollars to by her mourning.

To Rosettia Boon, negroes Catherine, Frederick and Jany, 3 feather beds, bedsteads and furniture, 1 walnut desk, cherry dining table and 100 dollars. And if she should die w/o heir then to her 3 brothers, Augustus Boon, George Boon and Nicholas Boon.

To Reverend Robert Angier, 20 dollars.

To Edward Jenkins my great waistcoat and pantaloons all ready made and my hat.

To William Acton, 10 dollars annually during his life paid by my brother Thomas B. Sansberrie.

To Edward Curtain, my great coat and one suit of my course clothes.

To Kitty Booth, a free woman of colour, the house where she now lives and the lot that is enclosed during her life, and then to my brother Thomas B. Sansberrie.

Item: it is my will and I do direct that the four children of Kitty Booth that is bound to me namely; Leonard, Amelia, George, and Ann, shall be released from bondage as they arrive to the year of maturity.

Item: my executors to examine my papers and if no receipt can be
found for one hogshead of tobacco which Leonard Mudd says is
yet due the heirs of Roswell Mudd for one years hire of negro
Ben, then I devise that they pay two hogsheads of tobacco to said
heirs within two years from my decease.

To brother Thomas B. Sansberrie all the residue of my estate both real
and personal, with this proviso only, that I reserve to my sister
Terecy Gwynn, in case Bennett Gwynn should dye first, the
privilege of making house where I now dwell her home at any
time and a sufficient support from my estate.

Executors: brother-in-law Bennett Gwynn and brother Thomas B.
Sansberrie

Signed: August 24, 1820   Isidere Sansberrie
Wit: James Robinson, Theodore Dyer, A. J. P. Boarman

Page 118.

Richard Bennett Pye, Will,   November 20, 1819; September 22, 1820

I, Richard Bennett Pye of CC, being in perfect health of body, and of
sound and disposing mind, memory and understanding;

To niece Sarah Mary Elizabeth Coursey and Aunt Ann Maria Mitchell
in conjunction, my plantation situate in Cornwallis Neck
containing 350 acres and in case of the death of my niece, it is my
desire the land descend to my Aunt and in the event of her death
to my Uncle James W. Mitchell during his natural life, when it is
my desire that it should devolve to my grandmother Elizabeth
Mitchell.

To Alexander Millar, the sum of 200 dollars.

Executrix: Aunt Ann Maria Mitchell

Signed: November 20, 1819   Richd B. Pye
Wit: Walter M. Millar, Ann Maria Millar, Thomas A. Burgess

Page 120.

Jane Contee, Will (copy),   January 5, 1820; June 3, 1820

I, Jane Contee of the town and county of Alexandria in the District of
Columbia;

To my slaves; Monaca, Nell, Anney & William, daughters and son of the
aforesaid Monaca, also Weston Hamilton and Philip Hamilton the
sons of the aforesaid Nell, their full and absolute freedom.

To John Contee and Richard Alexander Contee, the sons of my brother
Richard Alexander Contee, 1 guinea each.

To Matilda Margaret Snowden Sanders, Enoch Magruder and Richard
Alexander Contee Magruder, the daughter and sons of my sister

Ann Magruder, 1 guinea each.

To sister Elizabeth Keith, my half tract of land in Charles County Maryland, and conveyed to us jointly by our father .... (faded illegible writing was inserted between the line, but seems to suggest that after her death to her children) ...John Contee Keith, Elizabeth Contee Keith, Margaret Snowden Keith, Jane Ann Contee Keith and Catharine Contee Keith, the son and daughters of my sister.

To Elizabeth Contee Keith, Margaret Snowden Keith, Jane Ann Contee Keith and Catharine Contee Keith, the rest and residue of my estate.

Executors: sister Elizabeth Keith and James Keith Jr. her son

Signed: January 5, 1820　　　　　Jane Contee

Wit: John Roberts, John W. Massie, Thomas R. Keith, William Washington

At a session of the Orphans Court for the County of Alexandria, District of Columbia June 3, 1820 this last will and testament was presented my James Keith Jr. and proved in due form of law by the three subscribing witnesses and ordered to be recorded. Alexr Moore Reg Wills

Page 121.

Alexander Robey Sr., Will,　December 13, 1818; November 3, 1820

I, Alexander Robey of CC, being weak in body, but of sound and disposing mind, memory and understanding;

To son Elias Robey, the houses he now occupies and 2 acres of land around and above.

To two sons Heshijah {Hezekiah} Robey (during his natural life and then to Elias Robey) and Alexander Robey the whole of my real estate equally except for the above two acres.

To son Baruch Robey, 1 dollar.

To three grandchildren, Eliza Robey, Catharine Robey and Horace Robey, 1 dollar each.

Item: the rest and residue of my estate as follows; 1/4th to son Elias Robey, 1/4th part to daughter Cassandra's children to wit; Elenor Franklin, Adah Franklin, Sarah Franklin, William Robey Franklin, Alexander Franklin and Cassandra Franklin, 1/4th part to my daughter Chloe's children; William Thomas Robey and Sarah Robey, and remaining 1/4th part to my daughter Lucy Robey.

Executor: son Elias Robey

Signed: December 13, 1818　　　A Robey Senr

Wit: James Herbert, George H. Spalding, Daniel Carrington

Page 123.
John E. Carrington, Will, not dated; November 1, 1820
I, John E. Carrington of CC, being in perfect health of body and of sound and disposing mind, memory and understanding;
To grandmother Margaret Carnes, the hire or use of my negro Charles during her life and then to William H.C. Smith and case of his death to my sister Sarah Carrington.
To John and James Thompson the sons of James Thompson, the hire of my negro Smith for the benefit of their education and afterwards to my sister Sarah Carrington.
To William H.C. Smith, negro Celia and case of his death to my sister Sarah Carrington.
To William H.C. Smith, the balance of my estate real and personal for the use and benefit of his education.
Executor: none nominated
Signed: not dated   John E. Carrington
Charles County Sct., November 1, 1820. Then came James Garner in open court and made oath that the aforegoing instrument of writing to be the deceased will.

Page 124.
Francis Dunnington, Will, December 1, 1819; November 14, 1820
I, Francis Dunnington of CC, being in perfect health of body and of sound mind, memory and understanding;
To wife Margaret Dunnington, the use of 1/3 of my lands during her life and also 1/3 of stock of horses, cattle, sheep and hogs, negroes Harry Mudd, Joe, Cate, Henry, Horace, female child d/o Cate, 1 bed, bedstead and furniture, 1 bureau and 1 dozen windsor chairs.
To son Alexander Dunnington, all the land which I hold at my death. Also negroes; George, Bacchus, Jermes, all my stock of horses cattle, sheep and hogs, all my household and kitchen furniture, and plantation utensils, except the 1/3 bequeath to my wife.
To son Roger Dunnington, negro Dick.
To son Thomas Dunnington, negroes Rose and Nace.
To son Francis Dunnington, negro Jess.
To son Nathan Dunnington, negro Stephen.
To son John Brett Dunnington, negroes Valentine and Ben.
To son Hezekiah Dunnington, negroes Justin and Bob.
To daughter Henrietta Dunnington (wife of Walter Dunnington), negro Caroline.
To daughter Ann Brumel, negro Sarah.
To grandson Augustus Dunnington, (son of William P. Dunnington),

negro Austin.

To grandson Francis Dunnington, (son of William P. Dunnington), negro Dennis.

Executor: son Alexander Dunnington

Signed: December 1, 1819   Francis Dunnington

Wit: Samuel Hanson, Thomas M. Hanson, Gustavus Flowers

Charles County Sct., November 14, 1820. Then came Margaret Dunnington widow of Francis Dunnington who gave oath that the aforegoing instrument of writing was the true and whole last will and testament.

Page 127.

William Stone Jones, Will,   October 18, 1820; November 20, 1820

I, William Stone Jones of CC, being in a weak state of body, but of sound and perfect mind and understanding;

To brother Thomas Jones, 1 years services of my negro Charles Gray and then emancipated.

To negro George, his freedom at my decease.

To Miss Ann Thompson 200 dollars.

To Elizabeth Reeder, eldest daughter of Thomas H. Reeder, 200 dollars.

To brother Thomas Jones, in fee simple, all the residue of my estate real and personal, together with all bonds, notes, credits that may be due me.

Executor: brother Thomas Jones

Signed: October 18, 1820   Wm S. Jones

Wit: David Stone, James Brawner, Thomas H. Reeder

Page 128.

Hugh Perry, Will,   December 29, 1817; February 28, 1818

I, Hugh Perrie of CC, being infirm of body, but of sound mind and memory;

Imprimis, All my negroes to be set up to the highest bidder but not sold outside of my family.

To daughter Ann Perrie, a room in my house and as much land as she wishes to cultivate during her single life. Also my horse and choice of my cows. {negro} Jacob to cut wood for her. 1 feather bed and furniture, and bedstead and all my poultry. Also 1000 pounds crop tobacco, and 5 barrels Indian corn.

Item: it is my desire the chest of drawers, the large dining table, desk and dressing table to continue in the house that the son who belongs to the land, paying to the other children their equal parts.

Item: my land equally divided between sons James Perrie, Thomas D.
Perrie and Hugh Perrie
Executor: sons James Perrie and Thomas D. Perrie
Signed: December 29, 1817   Hugh Perry
Wit: John H. Thomas, Thomas B. Gibbons, William Turner Jr.

Page 130.
Susannah Edelen, Will,   November 19, 1818; December 8, 1818
I, Susannah Edelen of CC, being weak of body and of sound and
disposing mind, memory and understanding;
To daughter Elizabeth Edelen, negroes; Anthony and Seuly, 1 bed and
furniture, 1 desk and my large looking glass.
To son Lewis Edelen, negroes; Jack and Jude, 1 ox cart.
To son Edward Edelen, negroes; Mariah, Milly and Awzy.
To son John Horatio Edelen, negroes; Cryss and Sally and 100 dollars
cash.
Executor: son Lewis Edelen
Signed: November 19, 1818   Susannah Edelen
Wit: Thomas Burgess, Dennis Edelen, Ann M. Simpson

Page 132.
Edward Deakins Sr., Will,   September 25, 1816; January 3, 1821
I, Edward Deakins Sr. of CC, being weak, but of sound and disposing
mind, memory and understanding;
To son Edward Deakins, the whole of my lands, except 10 acres lying
on the Dressing Run.
To daughter Elenora Griffin, 100 dollars.
To daughter Margaret Williams, 100 dollars.
To daughter Annith Berry, 100 dollars.
To daughter Martha Hunt, 100 dollars.
To daughter Ann Robey, 100 dollars.
To six daughters; Elenora Griffin, Cecelia Reeves, Margaret Williams,
Annith {Asenath} Berry, Martha Hunt and Ann Robey all my
personal estate.
Executor: son Edward Deakins Jr.
Signed: September 25, 1816   Edward Deakins Sr
Wit: Henry Roberts, George H. Spalding, Charles Farrall

Page 134.
Ann Wood, Will,   January 2, 1821; January 30, 1821
I, Ann Wood of CC, being sick and weak of body, but of sound and
disposing mind and memory;
To son Giles G. Wood, 300 dollars for the benefit of his education and

taken out of the 1/3 personal estate which devolves to me by the death of my late husband Ignatius Wood deceased.

To three sons, Ferdinand F. Wood, William B. Wood, and Giles G. Wood the remainder of my estate.

Executor: William A. Tiar
Signed: January 2, 1821   Ann Wood
Wit: John B. Edelen, Charles A. Tier

Page 135.
John U{bgate} Cooke, Will,   April 10, 1820; January 30, 1821
I, John U. Cooke of CC, being sick and weak of body, but of sound disposing mind and memory;

To daughter Margaret Emery Turner, the negro girl Emerline I gave her at the time of her marriage with Edward Turner.

To son Jesse Cartwright Cooke negro Mary Ann.

To daughter Mary Pedder Cooke, negro Celia, 1 good bed and furniture, 1 other inferior one, 1 cow and yearling, 1 dish and a ½ dozen plates, 1 side saddle.

To wife Drucilla Cooke, all the remaining part of my property consisting of negroes, household and kitchen furniture, my stock of every description, plantation utensils, corn and provisions.

Executor: wife Drucilla Cooke
Signed: April 10, 1820   John U. Cooke
Wit: John B. Edelen, John W. G. Dixon

Page 136.
John Edward Fenwick, Will,   September 19, 1820; December 23, 1820
I, John Edward Fenwick of CC, being in a bad state of heath, but of sound memory and understanding;

To Charles A. Burnett of George Town, 25 dollars.

To Richard T. Simmes and Harper, 15 dollars between them.

To brother Robert Fenwick, negro Hellen.

To brother Joseph Fenwick, negro Alse.

To Reverend Mr. Francis Neale, 40 dollars.

To brother Alexander Leo Fenwick all the balance of my property.

Executor: brother Alexander Leo Fenwick
Signed: September 19, 1820   John E. Fenwick
Wit: Doctor Charles Lancaster, Robert Crain Jr.

Page 138.
Jesse Thomas, Will,   January 2, 1821; March 3, 1821
I, Jesse Thomas of CC;

To nephew Thomas Burch, my whole estate real and personal.

Executor: Edward Burch
Signed: January 2, 1821   Jesse Thomas
Wit: William B. Locke, Elkanah Moran, Thomas Carricoe

Page 139.
Mary P. Johnson, Will, November 22, 1820; March 3, 1821
I, Mary P. Johnson of CC, being sick and weak in body, but of sound and
    disposing mind, memory and understanding;
To Gustavus Johnson, a chest, one ax and 16 dollars cash.
To sister Matilda Smith, wife of Zachariah Smith, all and every part of
    the rest of my estate.
Executor: Zachariah Smith
Signed: November 22, 1820   Mary P. Johnson
Wit: John Moran Sr., Henry Davis

Page 140.
Margery Fowke, Will, November 1, 1819; March 6, 1821
I, Margery Fowke of CC, being weak of body, but of sound and
    disposing mind and memory;
To daughter Catharine Robertson, all my lands and real estate on
    condition that she convey unto the four children of my son
    Gerard Fowke in fee simple the proportion of the lands which
    she inherited of her father being part of Pointon Manor,
    commonly called Gunston. Also negro Albert, my carriage and
    horses, 1 large china bowl which belonged to her father, 1
    bottom counterpane, 1 ox cart and all the other utensils and
    implements of husbandry that may be on my farm at my death.
To daughter Sarah Brown, negroes; David, James, George (son of
    Diana), Clement, Harry, Henny, Alice & Maria.
To granddaughter Sarah Ann Caroline Brown, negroes Henry and
    Hester, and a bed and furniture.
To granddaughter Eleanor Brown, negro Nathan and a bed and
    furniture.
To granddaughter Catharine Brown (youngest daughter of my
    daughter Sarah), negro Dennis and a bed and furniture.
To grandson William Fowke son of James, at age 21 yrs, the following
    negroes; Daphne her children, William, Frederick, Spencer, Ann,
    Milly and Priscilla, to be held in trust by my son-in-laws Gustavus
    Brown and George Robertson.
To granddaughter Verlinda Stone Fowke, at age 21 yrs, negroes Peter
    and his tools, Herbert, Josias and Jude, to be held in trust by my
    son-in-laws Gustavus Brown and George Robertson. Also my bed
    and furniture and a bureau.

To grand children Mary Fowke, Catharine Fowke and William Augustus Fowke at age 21 yrs, negroes Alfred & Francis to Catharine Fowke, negroes Sarah and Richard her son to Mary Fowke, and negroes Ann and her son Jess to William Augustus Fowke, to be held in trust by my son-in-laws Gustavus Brown and George Robertson.

To daughters of son Gerard Fowke, a bed and furniture.

To granddaughter Mary Fowke a pair of mahogany tables and 1 dozen chairs now in the best room, in trust by my aforesaid trustees.

To grandson William Augustus Fowke, a large looking glass and horse cart, in trust by my aforesaid trustees.

To daughter Sarah, 1 large tumbler which was her fathers, a pair of sugar tongs, and a white cotton counterpane.

To granddaughters Mary and Catharine Fowke, all the rest and residue of my household and kitchen furniture including my table linen and towellry.

To daughters Sarah Brown (2/3) and Catharine Robertson (1/3), all the rest and residue of my estate (except 4 cows and 5 head of cattle to grandson William Augustus Fowke).

Item: son-in-law George Robertson to take care of and provide for at his own expense George, who is infirm.

Executors: son-in-laws Gustavus Brown and George Robertson

Signed: November 1, 1819   Margery Fowke

Wit: Henry H. Chapman, John Taylor, William R. Franklin

Page 145.

Mary Bowling, Will,   March 28, 1819; March 21, 1821

I, Mary Bowling of CC, being in sound mind, memory and understanding tho weak in health;

To niece Adeline Boarman, negro Teresa.

To nephew Joseph Boarman, negro John.

To niece Catharine Bowling, my right of negro Monicha, left me by Ann Sarah Queen.

To the priest serving this congregation at my death, 12 dollars.

To Reverend Mr. Charles Neale, 12 dollars.

To nephew Richard Bowling, the debt due me from brother Marsham Bowling.

To nephew John Boarman, my mare.

To nieces Ann, Catharine and Teresa, and nephew Austin Bowling the debt due me from them.

To niece Teresa Bowling 20 dollars.

To sister Eleanor Boarman the balance of my estate, requiring her to be particularly attentive to old man Gerard.

Executors: brother Marsham Bowling and brother-in-law John
    Boarman
Signed: March 28, 1819   Mary Bowling
Wit: Benjamin A. Lancaster, Roswell Harbin

Page 147.
Ann Smallwood, Will, November 7, 1815; May 1, 1821
I, Ann Smallwood of Prince George's County, being of good health and
    possessed of a good memory, judgment and understanding;
To daughter Emela {Amelia or Emily} Smallwood, all that I may die
    possessed of.
Executor: Emela Smallwood
Signed: November 7, 1815   Ann Smallwood
Wit: Peter Dejean

Page 148.
Aloysius Boarman, Will, October 16, 1786; May 30, 1821
I, Aloysius Boarman of CC, being of perfect health and memory;
To mother Mary Boarman part of tract "St. John's" lying in St. Mary's
    County during her natural life and then to my sister Elizabeth
    Boarman
To sister Elizabeth Boarman, if she should hold no part of the dwelling
    plantation where my mother now lives at her death, then I
    bequeath to my sister during her single life 100 acres of the
    above mentioned land.
To sister Mary Boarman, if she should hold no part of the dwelling
    plantation where my mother now lives at her death, then I
    bequeath to my sister during her single life 100 acres of the
    above mentioned land.
To brother Benedict Boarman the 200 acres if the above conditions
    are not met or my sisters marry or die before lawful age.
Executor: mother Mary Boarman and brother Benedict Boarman
Signed: October 16, 1786   Aloysius Boarman
Wit: William Chandler Brent, Joseph Semmes, Leonard Boarman Jr.

Page 150.
Edward Wheeler, Will, March 25, 1817; August 4, 1821
I, Edward Wheeler of CC, being in good health of body, and of sound
    and disposing mind and memory;
To niece Elizabeth Wheeler, d/o Josias and Barbary Wheeler, 1 feather
    bed and furniture.
To wife Hennariettar Wheeler, the residue of my property after debts.
Executor: none nominated

Signed: March 25, 1817   Edward Wheeler

Charles County Sct., August 4, 1821; then came Elizabeth Tubman and made oath that she was familiar with the hand writing of the deceased and believes this instrument of writing and is the same deposited it into her hands for safe keeping.

Page 151.

Teresa Welch, Will,   May 6, 1821; August 6, 1821

I, Tereza Welch of CC, being at this time in a low and weak state of health;

To son-in-law Edward Welch, son of my late husband Edward Welch, all my property.

Executor: son-in-law Edward Welch

Signed: May 6, 1821   Teresa Welch

Wit: Ann Clements, Ann Lawrence

Page 152.

Mary Fendall Cawood, Will,   February 15, 1821; August 14, 1821

I, Mary Fendall Cawood of CC, being in a low state of health but of perfect sound mind and memory;

To sister Charity Fendall Noble Hanson, negroes Fanny, Ann, Mary, Susan, and Ned during her life. Negro Ned to serve 9 years and then have his freedom and if my sister dies before this term, negro Ned to serve my nephew Doctor William Marshall the residue of his time.

To nephew Doctor William Marshall, negro Leo, and the aforesaid negro Annwith the proviso that he is not to bring any account against my estate.

To Elizabeth Fendall Hanson Marshall, d/o nephew Doctor William Marshall, negroes Fanny and Edward Henry, and 1 pair of silver sugar tongs.

To youngest daughter of nephew Doctor William Marshall, negro Maria.

To John Hancock Beans Marshall, s/o nephew Doctor William Marshall, negro John.

To nephew John Fendall Beall, negro Stephen.

To sister Margaret B. Beall, my side saddle.

To Elizabeth Margaret Hanson McPherson, d/o sister Elishabah B. McPherson, negro Clarisa, 1 small walnut table and 1 looking glass.

To Mary Margaret Hanson daughter of my brother Samuel Hanson, aforesaid negro Susan at the death of my sister Charity Fendall Noble Hanson.

To Prisy Hanson, d/o brother John B. Hanson, aforesaid negro Mary at
the death of my sister Charity Fendall Noble Hanson.
To Elizabeth Hanson Fendall McCubbin d/o niece Elizabeth Hanson
Fendall McCubbin, 1 bed and furniture.
To my three sisters; Margaret B. Beall, Elishabah B. McPherson and
Charity Fendall Noble Hanson, my part of the property left by my
father Samuel Hanson to his wife Sarah Hanson during her life.
Executors: nephews Doctor William Marshall and John Fendall Beall
Signed: February 15, 1821   Mary Fendall Cawood
Wit: Thomas B. Tubman, Thomas A. Davis

Page 155.
Ann Jameson, Will, not dated; August 15, 1821
I, Ann Jameson of CC, being at this time of sound disposing mind,
memory and understanding;
To sister Henrietta Jameson, my right to negro Charity and her son
Isaac, and the residue of my estate real personal or mixed.
Executor: sister Henrietta Jameson
Signed: not dated   Ann Jameson
Charles County Sct., August 15, 1821; then came John W. Smoot and
made oath that he was called on some time before Ann Jameson's
death by Martha Shierburn and Henrietta Jameson to write said
will. He was again called the day before her death and read the
same to her and she acknowledged it was written as she wished.

Page 156.
John Coffer, Will, May 23, 1816; August 17, 1821
I, John Coffer of CC, being sick and weak of body, but in perfect sense
disposing mind and memory;
Item: negro Harry to be hired out yearly and the money arising equally
divided between my three youngest daughters Elizabeth, Letticia
and Malinda for their support and schooling until they reach 16
years of age.
Item: the residue of my estate to be equally divided among the whole
of my representatives {not stated}.
Executor: not nominated
Signed: May 23, 1816   John Coffer
Wit: Hugh Cox, Robert Guest

Page 157.
William Stewart, Will, November 13, 1820; August 21, 1821
I, William Stuart of CC, being weak in body, but of sound and disposing
mind, memory and understanding;

To sons James Stuart and William Stuart all my real estate equally.
To son James Stuart, my colt.
To son John Stuart, negro Nell.
To sons James Stuart and William Stuart, all the remainder of the negroes.
To son William Stewart all the residue of my estate.
Executor: sons James Stuart and William Stuart
Signed: November 13, 1820   William Stuart
Wit: James Reeves, Henry L. Mudd, Nathaniel Hatton

Page 160.
Hebe Green, Will,   September 17, 1816; August 29, 1821
I, Hebe Green of CC, being sick and weak of body, but of sound and disposing mind, memory and understanding;
To mother Sarah Annis Atcheson all my negroes, vizt; Frank, Harriot, Smith and Elizaduring her life and then to her son William Hanson Atcheson.
Executor: mother Sarah Annis Atcheson
Signed: September 17, 1816   Hebe Green
Wit: William D. Beall, Isaac D. Beall

Page 162.
Horatio C. McEldery, Will,   September 2, 1821; October 9, 1821
I, Horatio C. McEldery of CC, being sick and weak of body, but of sound and disposing mind, memory and understanding;
Item: my executors to sell and dispose in fee simple my whole estate and the money arising invested in such profitable stock or funds for the use and benefit of my two infant children; Mary Elizabeth McEldery and John Patrick {McEldery} and paid at 21 yrs or marriage.
Item: negro Sophia, my old nurse set free and devise the occupation of the tenement whereon Harry Lewis now lives. Further, my executors to pay her 40 dollars annually during her life and that she take to live with her, her old father.
Item: my wife Eliza have full power and authority to manumit any of my slaves. Also her legal proportion and live on my estate in Charles County.
Executors: George Forbes, Hugh McEldery and Benjamin D. Higdon and wife Elizabeth McEldery
Signed: September 2, 1821   H.C. McEldery
Wit: James T. Johnson, William Latimer, John Winter

Page 164.
Catharine Campbell, Will,   May 7, 1821; October 9, 1821
I, Catharine Campbell of CC, being at present very sick, but of perfectly
    sound and disposing mind, memory and understanding;
To sister Judith Yates, negro Walter.
Item: whereas Daniel Jenifer, husband of my niece Eliza Trippe Jenifer
    is responsible for me for the payment of large sums of money, I
    bequeath the whole residue of my property to him.
Executor: Daniel Jenifer
Signed: May 7, 1821   Catharine Campbell
Wit: Eliza Winter

Page 165.
John Oakley, Will,   May 14, 1821; October 16, 1821
I, John Oakley of CC, being very sick and weak but in my natural
    reason;
To son Asa Oakley, 5 dollars.
To son Richard Oakley, 5 dollars.
To daughter Sary Learson {Lawson?}, 5 dollars.
To daughters Rebeccah Wilder, the residue of my estate.
Executor: not nominated
Signed: May 14, 1821   John Oakley
Wit: James G. Bateman, Hugh McMillan, Jane Bateman

Page 167.
Burdit Posey Sr., Will,   October 21, 1821; November 20, 1821
I, Burdit Posey Sr. of CC, being sick and weak of body, but of sound and
    disposing mind, memory and understanding;
To wife Dorothy, for and during the term of her natural life, the use of
    my negroes Peter and Amelia, all my household and kitchen
    furniture and such part of my stock of horses, cattle and sheep as
    may not necessarily be sold for the payment of my debts.
To son Burdit Posey, after the death of my wife the aforesaid negroes
    Peter and Amelia, 1 young black mare.
To two sons Francis Posey and John Posey, and my two daughters
    Elizabeth Posey and Sarah Posey, and my two granddaughters
    Sally Ann Posey and Ann Posey, the whole of the household
    furniture and stock after the death of my wife Dorothy.
Item: I direct that negro Harriet be sold and the money arising to be
    applied to the payment of the claim against me for the negroes
    purchased at the sale of the property of James Fowke deceased.
Executor: son Burdit Posey
Signed: October 21, 1821   Burdit Posey Sr.

Wit: J. D. Carpenter, William Hanson

Page 169.

Reverend John Weems, Will, October 16, 1821; December 7, 1821

I, John Weems of CC, being sick and weak in body, but of a sound and disposing mind, memory and understanding;

To son Charles S. Weems, the land I lived on, part of "His Lordships Favor" containing 196 acres. Also negro Charles (5 yrs old) s/o Alice.

To son George M. Weems, negroes Juliet (17 yrs old) and Jess the brother of Juliet (15 yrs old), Harriet d/o Alice (12 years old).

To son Lock Weems, negroes Alice and her two children, Ann & Kitty, John s/o Mary Ann (11 years old)

To daughter Sarah Ann Weems, in addition to the property I have already conveyed to her, my house servant Mary Ann (30 yrs old).

Item: I believe it is understood that one of the young negroes I conveyed to my daughter Sarah Ann turned out badly and I was obliged to sell her which note drawn by Henry Boswell in my favour for 475 dollars on August 29, 1818 I consider as her right.

To four youngest children; Charles, Mortimer, Lock and Sarah, those of my beds that have not been given away.

To son Charles, my present crop consisting of tobacco, rye, fodder and corn, also beef and pork sufficient for the support of the family for the ensuing year.

To two sons George Mortimer and Lock, all my stock of horses, cattle, sheep and hogs, and all my household and kitchen furniture not herein mentioned except my clock which I leave to son John.

To son James, all the debts which may be due me or coming to me from my brother's estate in Calvert and my gig together with a bed and furniture.

Executor: son Charles Weems.

Signed: October 16, 1821   John Weems

Wit: Elisha Robey, William Hunt, John A. Robey

Charles County Sct., December 7, 1821; then came James Isaac Weems and made oath that the aforegoing instrument of writing was delivered to him by the executor therein named to be exhibited for probate.

Page 171.

John Rowe Sr., Will, August 9, 1821; December 24, 1821

I, John Rowe Sr. of CC, being in a weak and low state of health, but of a sound disposing mind & memory;

To son George Rowe, the plantation I now live during his natural life, as he is in a weak and low state of health, at this death to be equally divided between his brother and sister, Polly J. Rowe and John Rowe.

Item: my personal property to be equally divided between my three children, son George Rowe, son John Rowe and daughter Polly J. Rowe.

To granddaughter Mary Ann Rowe, negro Milly.

To grandson George Marlow Rowe, negro Henry.

To granddaughter Sarah Elizabeth Rowe, negro Sally.

Executor: son George Rowe

Signed: August 9, 1821   John Rowe

Wit: John B. Ford, Walter W. Hannon, Leonard J. Farrall, Hezekiah Brawner

Page 173.

Zephaniah Franklin Sr., Will, September 23, 1820; January 2, 1822

I, Zephaniah Franklin Sr. of CC, being in perfect health and of sound and disposing mind, memory and understanding;

Imprimis; I do hereby confirm to all my children to whom I have heretofore made gifts of negroes and other property and which are now in their possession.

To son Zephaniah Franklin, the following tracts, "Mirey Branch", The Enlargement" and "Sandy Knowls" during his natural or single life and then to decend to my other children if he does not have lawful heir.

To grandson Francis Boucher Garrott, son of my daughter Ann Garrott, the land and plantation on which I now dwell, called "Winters Possession" including 50 acres of the same name I purchased of Richard Davis and Benjamin Burgess together with my mill and mill utensils in fee simple.

To my two granddaughters Harriot Franklin and Juliett Caroline Franklin, daughters of my deceased son John Downing Franklin, 800 dollars each.

To my granddaughters Sarah Young and Hannah Gray, daughters of my deceased son James Franklin, 1/4th part of my personal estate exclusive of other legacies and bequests equally divided.

To two daughters Priscilla Garrott and Ann Garrott, each 1/4th part of my personal estate exclusive of other legacies and bequests equally divided.

To my grandchildren, the sons and daughters of my deceased daughter Hannah Garrott, to wit; Middleton Garrott, Benedictor Cox or Cost, James Garrott and Barbara Garrott, 1/4th part of my personal estate exclusive of other legacies and bequests equally divided.

Item: my executors to sell and dispose of the following tracts; "Randalls" or "Randolphs Addition", "The Addition to Johnsons Beginning", "Moulds Venture", another part of "Randolphs Addition" I purchased of Nehemiah Franklin, "Widows Righted", "Come By Chance", and "Betsey's Delight", and the proceeds divided as follows; ¼ part to each of my daughters Priscilla Garrott and Ann Garrott, ¼ part to granddaughters Sarah Young and Hannah Gray equally, and the other 1/4ᵗʰ part to the children of daughter Hannah Garrott deceased.

Item: my executors to sell and dispose of my negroes and other personal property for the purpose of making distribution of the same as is herein before expressed.

Executor: Thomas Price Sr. and nephew Thomas Burgess

Signed: September 23, 1820   Zephaniah Franklin Sr.

Wit: Thomas Milstead, Henry McPherson of Henry, Nehemiah Crawford

Page 176.

Gustavus Gill, Will, November 2, 1821; January 12, 1822

I, Gustavus Gill of CC, being sick and weak in body, but of sound and disposing mind, memory and understanding;

To my three children, Charity Gill, Henry Gill and Elizabeth Gill all my land estate.

To daughter Charity Gill, negroes; Ben, Thom, Charles, Frank, Clary and Mary.

To son Henry Gill, negroes; Davy, Harry, William, Sook and Easter.

To daughter Elizabeth Gill, negroes; Abraham, George, Henny, Rachael, Lotty and Letty.

Executor: brother Roswell Gill (or in case he should not, then William Morton)

Signed: November 2, 1821   Gustavus Gill

Wit: Jesse Edwards, George W. Marriott, William Morton

Charles County Sct., January 12, 1822; then came Erasmus Gill the appointed Executor and made oath...

Page 178.

Henry Brawner Sr., Will & Codicil, October 16, 1817; January 12, 1822

I, Henry Brawner Sr. of CC, being of sound and disposing mind, memory and understanding;

To wife Esther Brawner, in lieu of her right of dower, and what the law entitles her to, 1/3 part of all my estate giving her the exclusive right of choosing the same so as to suit herself after an appraisement of and valuation of the same by two disinterested men, chosen by her and my children John, James and Henry.

To grandsons Henry Nelson and James Nelson, sons of my daughter Sarah Nelson, 100 dollars equally divided.

To daughter Ann Wood, negro Jenny now in her possession.

To daughter Catharine Dent, negro Louisa.

To son John Scott Brawner, negro Anna.

To son James Brawner, negroes Grace and Henny.

To son Henry Brawner, negro Ben.

Item: If I die possessed of any money, notes after debts, to be disposed of in the following manner; 1/3 to wife Esther Brawner, and the residue equally amongst children now here, to wit; John S. Brawner, James Brawner, Catharine Dent and Henry Brawner.

Item the residue of my estate after legacies to be equally divided amongst children, to wit; John S. Brawner, James Brawner and Henry Brawner and my two daughters Ann Wood and Catharine Dent.

Executor: not nominated

Signed: October 16, 1817   Henry Brawner

Wit: Thomas Price Sr., William Brawner

Codicil: the clause bequeathing to Henry Nelson and James Nelson is revoked, but if they shall be living and call for the same at any time previous to the division of my estate then they shall be only entitled to the legacy in said will mentioned.

Signed: not dated   not signed

Wit: Noble Young, James Brawner Jr., Basil Brawner

Charles County Sct., February 25, 1823; then came James Brawner Jr. one of the subscribing witnesses to the aforegoing codicil and made oath that he did see the testator sign and seal this codicil with Noble Young and Basil Brawner the other two subscribing witnesses.

Page 182.

George Hudson, Will,   November 7, 1821; January 18, 1823

I, George Hudson of CC, being sick and weak in body, but of sound and disposing mind, memory and understanding;

To daughter Ann Hudson, 1/3 part of all my estate.

To daughter Rebecca Hudson, 1/3 part of all my estate.

To wife Angelica Hudson, 1/3 part during her life and then to my two daughters.

Executrix: wife Angelica Hudson

Signed: November 7, 1821   George Hudson

44

Wit: Thomas Price Sr., Joseph Smoot, Ann R. Nelson

Page 184.
James Wheeler Sr., Will, January 29, 1821; February 12, 1822
I, James Wheeler of CC, being sick and weak in body, but of sound and
     disposing mind, memory and understanding;
To wife Darkey {Dorcas} Wheeler, 1/3 part of my property real
     personal or mixed and the balance divided amongst my children.
Executor: son James Wheeler
Signed: January 29, 1821   James Wheeler
Wit: Edward Simms, William Dent, Warren Burchel

Page 185.
Catharine C. Swann, Will, December 15, 1821; February 28, 1822
I, Catharine C. Swann of CC, being very sick and weak in body, but of
     sound, disposing mind, memory and understanding;
To sister Elizabeth Wilson, all my worldly goods.
Executor: George Robertson and Elizabeth Wilson
Signed: December 15, 1821   Catharine C. Swann
Wit: Hezekiah Dunnington, George Speake, Alexander Greer

Page 187.
Alexander Robey, Will, February 2, 1822; March 8, 1822
I, Alexander Robey of CC, being sick and weak in body, but of sound
     and disposing mind, memory and understanding;
To wife after debts and her thirds, the plantation whereon I now dwell
     containing 150 acres, and the use of all my personal estate
     during her natural life, and then to my six children; Henry Robey,
     Elizabeth Robey, Mary Robey, Uriah Robey, Malinda Robey and
     James Wilson Robey.
Executrix: wife Judith Robey
Signed: February 2, 1822   Alexander Robey
Wit: Stanislaus Murray, Hezekiah T. Dement, Hugh Murray

Page 189.
Priscilla Richards, Will, February 18, 1819; March 19, 1822
I, Priscilla Richards of CC, being of sound memory and judgment;
To son Leonard R. Richards, negroes; Lucy Sr. and Lucy Jr. , 4 head of
     cattle, 1 mare, 2 feather beds and furniture, 2 iron pots, 2 pair
     pot hooks, 1 dutch oven, 2 stone pots, ½ dozen soup plates, 2
     dishes, 1 table, 1 wheel, 1 pair pad irons, 1 pewter bason, 1 pr
     stilliards {portable scale}, 1 trunk and chest.
Item: one red cow and feather bed shall be sold to satisfy debts as well

as a note in my hands due from my son Gabriel Richards dated January 15, 1814 and due 6 months thereafter for the balance due from him to the paid estate of 73 dollars and 60 cents with interest thereon.

To son Gabriel Richards. 400 dollars.

To son Leonard R. Richards, negro Francis by paying son Gabriel Richards 400 dollars.

Executors: son Leonard R. Richards and Henry W. Hardy

Signed: February 18, 1819   Priscilla Richards

Wit: Sylvester F. Gardiner, Henry Padgett

Page 191.

Walter Winter Dunnington, Will, December 9, 1817; March 22, 1822

I, Walter Winter Dunnington of CC, being sick and weak in body, but of sound and disposing mind, memory and understanding;

To nephew George Dunnington, s/o Francis E. Dunnington, my land and plantation on which I now live called "The Park Enlarged", reserving the use, profits and occupation by my wife Henrietta Dunnington during her natural life. And if he should die before 21 yrs, then to his brother William Winter Dunnington.

To the other children of my brother Francis E. Dunnington, except the one who may inherit my land, the whole of my personal estate.

Item: my wife Henrietta Dunnington shall have all the property which came by her marriage to me to dispose of as she shall think proper.

Executors: wife Henrietta Dunnington and brother Francis E. Dunnington, and brother-in-law Thomas Dunnington.

Signed: December 9, 1817   Walter Winter Dunnington

Wit: Thomas Price Sr., Josephus Brummet, William Greer

Page 194.

Thomas S. Brawner, Will, March 30, 1822; April 23, 1822

I, Thomas S. Brawner of CC, being very sick and weak of body, but of perfect sound mind and memory;

To my nephew John A. Maddox and niece Eleanor Maddox jointly, my dwelling plantation whereon I now live, part of a tract called "Wentworths Woodhouse" 194 acres.

Item: all the residue of my lands and as much of my other personal property except sundry negroes herein after mentioned, should be sold to close the whole of my debts.

Item: to friend Robert Brawner, the control and management of my mulatto boy Lawson to be bound out to some good trade until 21 yrs and then freed.

Item: to friend Robert Brawner, the control and management of my mulatto girl Cinthia until16 yrs and then freed.

Item: to friend Robert Brawner, the control and management of my negro woman Dolly and her four children, Jefferson, Caroline, Herbert and Washington, the boys bound at some good trade at 16 yrs and serve till 21 yrs and then set free and the negro mother Dolly set free when negro girl Caroline reaches 16 yrs.

To Joseph Maddox's, Benjamin Berry's and Henry Brawner's children, my nephews and nieces, the remaining part of my estate.

Executors: friends Robert Brawner, Henry Brawner and Benjamin Brawner

Signed: March 30, 1822   Thos S. Brawner

Wit: Frederick Nelson, Noah Brawner, Jane Thorn

Page 196.

Thomas Jenkins, Will,   March 20, 1822; May 21, 1822

I, Thomas Jenkins of CC, being of sound disposing mind and memory;

To son Henry Jenkins, negroes; Gusta, Mary, Teresa and Susan, estimated by me at 720 dollars.

To son William Jenkins, negroes; Andrew, Jane, Charles Ned, Mary and Bett, estimated at 920 dollars.

To son Felix Jenkins, negroes; Alexius and Ben, estimated at 600 dollars.

To son Benedict Jenkins, negroes; George, Mary, Henny and Helen, estimated at 1350 dollars.

To son Frederick Jenkins, negroes; Allen and James, estimated at 800 dollars.

To son Lewis A. Jenkins, negro Joseph, estimated at 450 dollars.

To daughter Eliza Jenkins, negroes; Harriet, Elenor, Ralph, Meada, Henny and Nace, estimated at 920 dollars.

To daughter Mary Matilda Semmes, negroes; Teresa, Henny, Toney, Alexius, Olevia and Henny, estimated at 1540 dollars.

To the trustees of the Cobb Neck Church, 50 dollars.

Item: To all my children, Henry, William, Felix, Benedict, Frederick, Lewis, Eliza, and Mary Matilda the plantation I now live on and it is my desire that it should be sold on credit, 2 to 3 years, the purchasers giving bods with sufficient security.

Item: The proceeds from the sale of my real estate together with the residue of my personal property including the estimated value of the negroes hitherto delivered to my children shall be summed up and divided into ten equal parts and that my daughters Eliza and Mary Matilda, shall draw two parts each out of the sum.

Item son Lewis A. Jenkins sole executor recommending him to consult

and advise with Thomas A. Davis and John Jenkins Esq. whenever necessary.
Executor: son Lewis A. Jenkins
Signed: March 20, 1822   Thomas Jenkins
Wit: John H. Lancaster, Michael Boarman, Charles J. Lancaster

Page 199.
Hezekiah Berry, Will,   March 14, 1822; July 9, 1822
I, Hezekiah Berry of CC, being in poor health of body, but of sound and disposing mind, memory and understanding;
To son Hepburn S. Berry, slave Henrietta who I wish to be well treated and taken care of for her fidelity to me.
To my three children, Hepburn S. Berry, George M. Berry and Emily A. Mudd, wife of Francis L. Mudd, all the rest of my estate
Executor: sons Hepburn S. Berry and George M. Berry
Signed: March 14, 1822   Hezekiah Berry
Wit: Philip J. Ford, Francis Cox, John Turner

Page 201.
Sarah Knott, Will,   June 6, 1822; August 8, 1822
I, Sarah Knott of CC, being sick and weak of body, but of sound and disposing mind, memory and understanding;
To daughter Ann Mattingly, negro William during her natural life and then to Sidney Ann Mattingly the d/o said daughter Ann Mattingly. Also negro John, 1 bed and bedstead and furniture.
To son-in-law Edward Mattingly, in trust, negroes Rachael and George, the profits arising to be annually paid to my daughter Sarah Johnson wife of Walter Johnson during her life and after her death to her children.
To grandson Alexander Johnson, 1 mare colt.
To grandson George Washington Talbot {Talburtt}, negroes Harry and Margaret.
Item: there is now a sum of money belonging to me (about 500 dollars) deposited in one of the banks of Washington City by my son-in-law Edward Mattingly, and which is the proceeds of the sale of certain negroes I formerly loaned to my daughter Cecelia Devaughn, now I give and bequeath the said sum unto my son-in-law Edward Mattingly in trust and applied to the purchase of a negro or negroes for the use of my daughter Cecelia Devaughn and after her death to her children.
To son Charles Knott, 1 cow and calf, 1 bed, bedstead and furniture, and it is my wish and desire that his children should receive whatever may be the fair value of my house and lot situated near

the public road and near the junction of the roads leading from Allens Fresh and Piccawaxon to Port Tobacco and now occupied and used as a school house. I hereby charge my son John Knott with the payment of the fair value of the house and lot, 12 months after my death.

To grandson Charles Knott, 1 heifer.

To granddaughter Harriet Knott, the bed, bedstead and furniture which I use.

Item: my servant Anthony shall be sold by my executor and the money arising divided between my grandchildren Harrison Knott and George Knott and the children of my son John Knott and of my son Charles Knott.

To daughter-in-law, Louisa Knott wife of John Knott, all my wearing apparel to be divided between her own children, Charles Knott's children and Elizabeth Knott's children.

To son Charles Knott, an ox cart now in his possession.

To son John Knott, the plantation or tract of land on which I now live, and the rest and residue of my estate subject to the payment of all my just debts.

Executor: son John Knott

Signed: June 6, 1822   Sarah Knott

Wit: William D. Merrick, Richard T. Penn, Michael Maloney

Linda Reno note: Jane, daughter of Sarah Knott m. Lewin Talburtt (d. 1831 Washington DC)

Page 205.

Leonard Mudd, Will & Codicil,   January 27, 1822; August 21, 1822

I, Leonard Mudd of CC, being weak of body, but of sound and disposing mind, memory and understanding;

To son William Mudd at 21 yrs, his choice of my two plantations, the one on which I now live composed of "Reuden Jenkins Poor Chance", "Addition to Jenkins Poor Chance". The other whereon George Dyer now lives composed of "St. Catharine".

To daughters Beatrice Mudd, Caroline Mudd and Clarecy Mudd, the rest and residue of my lands when son William has made his choice.

To daughter Mary Eliza Mudd, negroes Marger and her two children Ann and Sam, and Sandy, which 4 negroes are in the employment of my brother-in-law William Gardiner, and whereas he now holds my note for a certain sum of money on which I claim a credit of 170 dollars, a payment made, now the condition of the above legacy is that if the credit not be given my executors to detain so much of the legacy as would make good the payment.

To the priest that may be in this congregation at the time of my death, 15 dollars that he may say masses for me and my two departed wives.

To the heirs of David Slater, 13 pounds current money with interest from the date of an account against Henry Hagan on said Slaters books of eighteen or twenty years standing.

To sister-in-law Elizabeth McWilliams, whatever balance appears to be due.

To my four children, William Mudd, Beatrice Mudd, Caroline Mudd, and Clarecy Mudd all the rest and residue of my estate.

Item: my sister-in-law Elizabeth McWilliams to have a home and board with my daughters if she chooses.

Item: in case my daughter Mary Eliza Mudd should be in distress or want of a home, she should be received and provided for by my other children.

Item: My executors to comfortably clothe and feed my two aged slaves, Ralph and Agness.

Item: I desire my son William be entirely under the control and guardianship of Benedict J. Heard of St. Mary's County.

Executors: Benedict J. Heard of St. Mary's County and William Gardiner of Charles County

Signed: January 27, 1822   Leonard Mudd

Wit: Theodore Mudd, George Dyer, Josias Hamilton

Codicil: whereas 25 or 26 years ago I purchased of Joseph Miles several tracts of land , about 22 acres of which appeared not to have sufficient title, in consequence I withheld a part of the purchase money and have lately employed an attorney at law to procure me a good title and when procured the heirs of the said Miles should be paid a just amount with interest.

Signed: January 27, 1822   Leonard Mudd

Wit: Theodore Mudd, George Dyer, Josias Hamilton

Page 210.

Randolph Turner, Will, March 5, 1816; August 27, 1822

I, Randolph Turner of CC, being in perfect health of body and mind;

To wife Elizabeth Turner, the use of all my estate both real and personal during her natural life or widowhood and then to my unmarried daughters during their single lives but as soon as they are married, they are no longer entitled, but the entire right, title and privilege of the whole of my real estate is to be and remain unto my son Aquila Turner.

Executor: son Aquila Turner

Signed: March 5, 1816   Randolph Turner

Wit: Samuel Turner, John Farrand, Jesse C{artwright} Cooke

Page 212.

Joseph King, Will,   June 15, 1822; August 27, 1822

I, Joseph King of William and Mary's Parish of CC, being at this time in good health and of perfectly sound and disposing mind, memory and understanding;

To daughters of Stephen Latimer late of CC deceased; Ann Elizabeth Latimer, Louisa Latimer, Sarah Rebecca Latimer and Mary Latimer, the whole of my estate, real and personal as tenants in common and not as joint tenants.

Executor: Hannah Elizabeth Latimer (widow and relict of Stephen Latimer)

Signed: June 15, 1822   Joseph King

Wit: John Campbell, John B. Hanson, Matilda C. Johnson

Page 213.

Sarah Coomes, Nucuputive {Oral} Will,   September 10, 1822; September 12, 1822

The dying request of Sarah Cooms that a negro girl named Eliza shall be the property of Eleanor Cooms with all the rest of her property, excepting a man named Ned, negro woman Harriott and child which she gives to her sister Jane Hamilton's children.

Charles County Sct., September 12, 1822; then came Stanislaus Cooms, Sally Lovelace and Eleanor Ferrol and severally made oath that they were present when they heard Sarah Cooms deceased on the 10th instant, declare that the words reduced to writing in the aforegoing instrument was her last will and she requested each of the witnesses to take notice that the words as therein contained was her last will.... And the words spoken was in the house wherein she had resided all her life and reduced to writing the evening the deceased departed this life.

Page 214.

John Baptist Edelen, Will,   March 22, 1819; October 3, 1822

I, John Baptist Edelen of CC, being sick and weak of body, but of sound mind and understanding;

To son John Henry Edelen, 60 dollars for the benefit of his education.

To wife Helena Edelen, 1/3 part of my estate.

To my four children, Harriot Clarke, Stanislaus Edelen, Mary Henrietta Kirk and Dennis Edelen, the other 1/3 part of my estate.

To all my children, Harriot Clark, Stanislaus Edelen, Mary Henrietta Kirk, Dennis Edelen, Sarah Ann Edelen and John Henry Edelen,

the other 1/3. And whereas I give to my daughter Harriot Clark at the time of her marriage, negro Liddy valued at 250 dollars and this is to be considered as so much received of her dividend.
Joint Executors: brother Joseph Edelen and William McAtee half-brother to my wife.
Signed: March 22, 1819   John Baptist Edelen
Wit: Ignatius Wood, Edward Edelen

Page 216.
Sarah Green, Will, August 6, 1822; November 4, 1822
I, Sarah Green of CC, being sick and weak of body, but of sound and disposing mind, memory and understanding;
To daughter Sarah Murray, 1 black walnut desk.
To son Henry Green, 50 dollars.
To Reverend Mr. Eaih, 15 dollars.
To daughter Jane Wills, the residue of my property.
Executor: Charles Wills
Signed: August 6, 1822   Sarah Green
Wit: Eleanor Wathen, Wilson Smoot

Page 218.
Thomas Price Sr., Will, June 2, 1822; November 5, 1822
I, Thomas Price Sr. of CC, being in perfect health of body, but of sound and disposing mind, memory and understanding;
To son Thomas Price, part of tract "the Addition" which I purchased of Hezekiah Elgin, lying on the west side of the Spring Branch, also part of a tract called "Bretts Discovery" which I purchased of William William Dent and his sisters to begin in the first line when it crosses the road now leading from Nanjemoy Church. Also negroes; Jim and Mary now in his possession and confirm all the stock, furniture and plantation utensils I have heretofore given him and exonerate him from all money loaned him or paid by me for the land deed to him by Thomas H. Reeder.
To daughter Elizabeth Gray, tract "Kennedy's Marsh" and "Brawners Resurvey", which I purchased of William Kennedy. Also mullato Nancy and confirm the stock, furniture I have heretofore given her.
To daughter Mary Dunnington, part of tract "Remainder" and tract "Any Thing" which I purchased of William Kennedy, and three other parts of tracts purchased from Levi Scott called "The Remainder", Partners Mistake", and "Ignorance Passion". Also negro Eliza in her possession and confirm the stock, furniture I have heretofore given her.

To executors in trust for my daughter Catharine Garrott in fee simple forever tracts "Grays Addition", "Grays Purchase" and "Brett's Good Chance", which I purchased of Francis Evans, James G. Evans and Levi Scott. Also negro Dianna 1 black horse, 2 cows and calves, 6 head of sheep, 2 young sows and 10 pigs, 1 bed and furniture, 6 chairs and the kitchen utensils.

To daughter Henrietta Price, tracts "Elgins Discovery", part of "Batchelors Agreement" which I purchased of William A. Elgin. Also negro Sidney, a horse, 2 cows, 6 sheep, 1 bed and furniture called hers, ½ dozen silver teaspoons, 1 pair silver sugar tongs, 1 sow and 6 shoats.

To son John Francis Price, the land and plantation I now live on called "Robertsons Purchase Resurveyed", also the residue of tract "The Addition", except the mill and the mill dam, also the residue of tract "Bretts Discovery" which I purchased of William Dent and his sisters, reserving nevertheless to my wife Catharine Price the use and benefit of said lands together with my mill and its profits for her support during her life jointly with son John Francis Price and a home and support for my daughter Henrietta Price during her single life. Also negroes; Harry and Lizza, 1 bay horse, 2 yoke of oxen, an ox cart, 2 cows, 6 sheep, 8 young hogs, 1 mahogany desk, 1 walnut bureau, 1 walnut dining table, 1 bed and furniture, my small gun, 6 table spoons.

To sons Thomas Price and John Francis Price, at the death of my wife, my mill and mill dam as tenants in common.

Item: my executors to sell negro Hendley for the purpose of discharging said debts.

Executor: sons Thomas Price Jr. and John Francis Price

Signed: June 2, 1822   Thos Price Sr.

Wit: Robert Ferguson, Robert Gray, Humphrey Cobey

Page 223.

Raphael Jameson, Will,   August 23, 1822; November 12, 1822

I, Raphael Jameson of CC, being in perfect health of body, and of sound and disposing mind, memory and understanding;

To daughter Catharine S. Langley, 50 dollars in addition to what she has already received.

To daughter Sarah Q Edelen, 50 dollars in addition to what she has already received.

To daughter Letitia Lancaster, 50 dollars in addition to what she has already received.

To son Benjamin H. Jameson, my dwelling plantation ... betwixt my brother Samuel Jameson and myself which land was purchased of the heirs of John Edelen deceased, with the exception of my dwelling house and out house. Also parcel of land lying in the neighborhood of Burch's mill and belonging equally between Samuel Jameson, the heirs of Thomas Jameson deceased, and myself.

To daughters Elizabeth A. Jameson and Jane C. Jameson, all the residue of my plantation laying on the east and south side, with the privileges of ½ my dwelling house, out houses, and garden spring, etc, during their single life and after death or marriage to devolve to son Benjamin H. Jameson.

Executrix: daughter Elizabeth A. Jameson

Signed: August 23, 1822   Raphael Jameson

Wit: Edward Edelen Sr., Nicholas Mills, Luke F. Jameson

Page 226.

Eleanor Canter, Will, October 17, 1822; November 15, 1822

I, Eleanor Canter of CC, being very weak in body, but of perfect mind and memory;

To daughter Elizabeth Canter's 7 children; Mary Canter, Lettice Canter, Catharine Canter, Eliza Harriet Canter, John Alexander Canter, Robert Canter, Ann Morris Canter, negroes; Pricey and Henry.

To granddaughter Mary Canter, 1 dark gray colt.

To son Robert Lyon, negroes Daniel and Charity.

To son Horatio Canter, negro Vine, 1 light gray mare, 1 gray horse, 1 yoke of steers, 1 ox cart, 1 brindle cow, all my plantation utensils, 1 new bed and furniture, 1 oval table and table cloth, 1 large iron pot and hooks, 1 frying pan, 1 tea kettle, 1 large stone pot, 1 small stone pot, the present or last crop of corn, fodder, rye, oats and tobacco and 500 weight of pork.

To sons Robert Lyon and Horatio Canter, a tract purchased by me of Elijah Canter lying on the left side of the road leading from Benedict to Bryantown after their paying 60 dollars to each of my 3 children; Elizabeth Canter, Lydia Musgrove Moran and Henry Canter.

Item: All other property, money on hand, all moneys due me after burial expenses and debts to be equally divided between my 5 children; Elizabeth Canter, Robert Lyon, Lydia Musgrove Moran and Henry Canter and Horatio Canter.

Executor: not nominated

Signed: October 17, 1822   Eleanor Canter

Wit: Erasmus Gill, Gustavus Cartwright, Samuel Cartwright

54

Page 228.
Heland Edelen, Will, October 29, 1822; November 26, 1822
I, Heland {Helena} Edelen of CC, being sick and weak in body, but of
    sound and disposing mind, memory and understanding;
To daughter Sarah Ann Edelen, 100 dollars.
To son John Henry Edelen, ½ of my undivided thirds of my husband
    John B. Edelen's estate.
To daughter Sarah Ann Edelen, the other ½ of my undivided thirds of
    my husband estate.
Item: if both son and daughter die before lawful age and w/o heir, then
    to my brother William McAtee.
Executor: half-brother William McAtee
Signed: October 29, 1822   Heland Edelen
Wit: Thomas Burgess, Horatio Edelen, Grace Edelen

Page 230.
Thomas Andrew Davis Sr., Will, October 1, 1822; December 7, 1822
I, Thomas Andrew Davis of CC, being sick and weak in body, but of
    sound disposing mind, memory and understanding;
To cousin Elizabeth Ann Dyson, negroes Maria and Henry, 1 horse,
    bridle and saddle, 4 head of cattle, 1 bed and furniture and 100
    dollars cash. Also negro Nace. These bequeaths are to be
    considered in lieu of and in bar of any claim which she might or
    could have against me on account of any property which might
    have come into my hands on account of her mother's estate.
To son Thomas Andrews Davis Jr., negro Tom.
To Mrs. Stewart the widow of the late Francis Ignatius Stewart, 1 lot
    or piece of ground where he formerly lived and which was
    purchased by me at Sheriffs sale.
To wife Elizabeth Grace Davis, the rest and residue of my estate and
    all my children, vizt; Thomas A. Davis, Elizabeth Ann Davis,
    Samuel Dyson Davis, Henrietta Davis, Mary Grace Davis, and Ann
    Amanda Davis.
Executrix: wife Elizabeth Grace Davis
Signed: October 1, 1822   Tho A. Davis
Wit: Alexander Matthews, William Hamilton, Morgan Harris

Page 232.
Mary Gray, Will, September 19, 1821; December 30, 1822
I, Mary Gray of CC, being in a low state of health, but of sound and
    disposing mind, memory and understanding;
Item: my stock, household furniture, plantation utensils and crop
    should be sold and applied to the payment of my debts. If it is not

sufficient, negro Bill should be sold.
Item: freedom for all my negroes (except Bill), namely; Nance, George, John, Galen, Jeremiah, Luecy, Dolly, Sarah, Ann and Sophia.
Executor: friend Francis Elgin Dunnington
Signed: September 19, 1821   Mary Gray
Wit: Alexander Murdock, Gilbert Barker

Page 234.
Francis Edelen Sr., Will,   May 18, 1822; January 17, 1823
I, Francis Edelen Sr. of CC, being weak of body, but of sound mind and memory;
To wife Martha Edelen, negroes; Jerry, Sarah, Menter, Hendley, Josias, Frank, Lewis, William and James forever, except James to nephew Harwood Edelen, son of Jeremiah Edelen.
To wife Martha Edelen all the land whereon I now live being part of tract "Greens Inheritance" laying on Port Tobacco branch and on the south side containing 60 acres.
Executor: wife Martha Edelen
Signed: May 18, 1822   Francis Edelen
Wit: Joseph Green, Stanislaus Coomes, Francis C. Green

Page 236.
Lucy Mudd, Will,   December 25, 1822; January 18, 1823
I, Lucy Mudd of CC, being sick and weak in body, but of a sound and disposing mind;
To Maria Wills, daughter of Joseph J. Wills, 1 bed and furniture.
To Lucy Ann Wills, daughter of Joseph J. Wills, 1 bed and furniture.
To Leucresia Ann Simms, daughter of Francis Simms, 1 red cherry table and 1 side saddle.
To Lucinda Ann Simms, daughter of Francis Simms, 1 red cherry table and 1 side saddle.
To sister Eleanor Simms children, the remaining part of my property.
Executrixes: nieces Leucresia Ann Simms and Lucinda Ann Simms
Signed: December 25, 1822   Lucy Mudd
Wit: William Hanson McPherson Garner, Walter B. Padgett, Daniel Smallwood

Page 238.
Catharine Chapman Laidler, Will,   August 30, 1821; January 22, 1823
I, Catharine Chapman Laidler of CC, being in perfect health of body, and of sound and disposing mind, memory and understanding;
To my three sisters, Mary Ann Laidler, Eleanor Laidler and Jane Barnes Laidler, as tenants in common, all my estate both real

personal and mixed.
To sister Violetta B. Jamison, 50 dollars for purchasing a full suit of
mourning.
Executrixes: sisters, Mary Ann Laidler, Eleanor Laidler and Jane
Barnes Laidler
Signed: August 30, 1821   Catharine C. Laidler
Wit: Jazarael Hoskins Hanson Penn, William H. Penn, Richard
Thompson Penn

Page 240.
Horatio Smoot, Will, December 14, 1822; February 22, 1823
I, Horatio Smoot of CC, being in sound state of mind, but of feeble and
weak state of body;
To single daughters an equal share in my landed estate so long as they
remain in a state of celibacy, should they marry, then my sons to
have property.
Item: It is my wish that my sons by my last wife shall have a common
English education and then bound out to some trade.
Executor: not nominated
Signed: December 14, 1822   Horatio Smoot
Wit: Arthur Latimer, Elkanah Swann, Thomas Scrivner

Page 241.
Philip Gardiner, Will, February 7, 1822; March 4, 1823
I, Philip Gardiner of CC, being sick and weak in body, but of sound and
disposing mind, memory and understanding;
To my brother-in-law Joseph A. Gardiner all my negroes; Davy
(carpenter), Monaca, Jenny, Day (15 yrs) and Sharlott, Also negro
Henry in possession of Walter Cooke, and my wearing apparel.
To sister Elizabeth Gardiner 100 dollars.
To Reverend Mr. Angier, 20 dollars.
To Reverend Mr. Francis Neale, 10 dollars.
To Reverend Mr. Murfee who attends Mattawoman congregation, 10
dollars.
To Reverend Mr. Mathas of St. Patrick's Church, City of Washington,
10 dollars.
The intention of the bequeaths to these several Reverend gentlemen
is that prayers may be offered up to the Almighty God for the rest
of my soul agreeable to the [blank] of the Roman Catholic Church.
Executor: brother-in-law Joseph A. Gardiner and sister Elizabeth
Gardiner
Signed: February 7, 1822   Philip Gardiner
Wit: John Gardiner, George Gardiner, John Bignell

Page 243.
Samuel Collins, Will, September 10, 1822; February 4, 1823
I, Samuel Collins of CC, being of memory and disposing mind;
To wife Mary Ann Collins, all my real and personal property during
her single life and at her death or remarriage, my two tracts of
land "Thomas Maggot" and "Thomas Adventure" whereon I now
reside to be divided between my two sons Henry Collins and
William Collins. Son Henry to have the east end beginning in the
Beaver Dam line of said tracts, 10ft eastward of a cabin
commonly called Old Ralphs Cabin standing by a spring called
the Locust Spring, running to the dividing line between the land
of Major Henry S. Yates (which property belonged to Major John
C. Jones) and son William the remaining part which will include
my dwelling house. In the event of son Harry's death without
lawful issue, to daughter Jane, and in the event of son William's
death without an heir, to daughter Eleanor.
In the event of my wife's death or remarriage, I bequeath to my
daughters Mary Collins, Jane Collins and Eleanor Collins during
their single lives, 6 acres of land beginning at the Gum Spring and
running in a straight line through Capt. William Farr's graveyard
so as to include a piece of marsh and the old orchard. Also
enough timber to build a comfortable house from the lands left
to my son Henry.
Executor: Mary Ann Collins
Signed: September 10, 1822   Samuel Collins
Wit: Josias Hawkins, James G. Bateman, Richard Ratcliff

Page 246.
Esther Brawner, Will & Codicil, February 21, 1822; March 19, 1823
I, Esther Brawner of CC, being sick and weak of body, but of a sound
and disposing mind, memory and understanding;
To niece Ann Brummit, negro Jenney.
To Rebecca Dunnington, d/o John P. Dunnington, negro Doll.
To John Dunnington, s/o John P. Dunnington, negro Sarah Ann.
To niece Kitty Murdock, negro Kitty.
To two nieces Peggy Dunnington and Precius Dunnington, equally,
negro Nancy.
To Alexander Dunnington, negro Clodius.
To Peter Dunnington, negro Isaac.
Executor: Francis E. Dunnington
Signed: February 21, 1822   Esther Brawner
Wit: John S. Brawner, Peter Rison
Codicil: In addition of what I have bequeath to my niece Precius

Dunnington, a young mare and my saddle, and my wearing apparel divided among my relations as she may please.

Signed: January 7, 1823   Esther Brawner

Wit: Francis E. Dunnington, John S. Brawner

Page 249.

Thomas C. Clements, Will, April 3, 1822; March 25, 1823

I, Thomas C. Clements of CC, being low in health but of sound mind and perfect memory and understanding;

To wife Elizabeth S. D. Clements, all my real and personal property during her natural life with the exception of the following negroes; Sandy, John, Bill and Jess, Louisa, Maria and Ann, which negroes I bequeath to my daughter Mary Ann Elizabeth when she arrives at age.

Item: should my wife and daughter both die unmarried, then all my property shall be equally divided amongst my brothers and sister after my brother John H. Clements has first received out of my estate 1000 dollars.

Item: The negroes that which came in marriage by my wife shall revert back to her own relations.

Executor: wife Elizabeth S. D. Clements

Signed: April 3, 1822   Thomas C. Clements

Wit: Benjamin T. Dulany, Leonard J. Farrall, Francis C. Green

Page 250.

William B. Smoot, Will & Codicil, August 26, 1822; April 17, 1823

I, William B. Smoot of CC, being weak in body, but of sound and disposing mind, memory and understanding;

To daughter Letitia Hanson Smoot, 1/3rd part of the plantation on which I at present reside and include my dwelling house, one house and improvements. Also negroes; John, Little Charles, Delia, Anna (cook), Harriet and her child Priscilla, and Little Nancy. Also, my gelding, riding gig and harness, 1 feather bed and furniture.

To two sons William Hoskins Smoot and John Smoot, all the rest and residue of my dwelling estate being 2/3rds part as tenants in common and equally divided.

To son Walter Hanson Smoot, tract of land purchased from Robert Edelen containing 230 acres, also negroes; Tom, Evelina and her child Malvina, Charles (carpenter), Dodson and Susan.

To son Hanson Smoot, 50 acres of land, part of tract "George's Rest", whereon Edward Ford at present resides, and tracts "The Bridges" and "Smoots Triangle". Also negroes, Alice, Old Milly,

Jack, Carlotte and Flora.

To son William Hoskins Smoot, negroes; Jess, Mary and her child Ben Turner, Young Milly, Maria d/o Mary, and Henry.

To son John Smoot, negroes; Chloe, Cato, Betty, Peggy, Jerry and Warren.

To two granddaughters, Elizabeth Eleanor Briscoe and Mary Letitia Briscoe at 16 yrs, negroes; Henny and her child Tabitha.

Executor: To son Walter Hanson Smoot and friends Alexander Matthews and John Edelen of the town of Port Tobacco.

Signed: August 26, 1822   William B. Smoot

Wit: Mary H. Muschett, John T. Dyson, William Hendly Smoot

Codicil: Whereas I did not give my son Doctor Charles Smoot any property, I now give him negroes; Susan, Betty, Young Milly and Frederick. Also 1/6ᵗʰ part of the residue of my personal estate.

Signed: October 11, 1822   William B. Smoot

Wit: Eleanor Smoot, Peggy B. Smoot, Mary H. Muschett

Page 255.

Joshua Montgomery, Will, June 10, 1821; April 29, 1823

I, Joshua Montgomery of CC, being in tolerable health and sound memory;

To son Joseph Caleb Montgomery, negro John Baptist provided he come in person to receive him. Otherwise to my three children Henry Montgomery, Catharine Montgomery and Alley Montgomery.

To son Henry Montgomery, negro Raphael.

To daughter Catharine Montgomery, negroes; Francis, Augustine, Dominic, Patrick, Mary and Susan, and 1 feather bed and furniture.

To daughter Alley Montgomery, negroes; Moses, Benedict and Francis Hilery, and 1 feather bed and furniture.

To daughters Catharine and Alley during their single lives, negro Charity and at the end of that term, freed.

Executor: son Henry Montgomery

Signed: June 10, 1821   Joshua Montgomery

Wit: Martha Osburn, William Morton

Page 257.

Draden Waters, Will, February 19, 1822; May 7, 1823

I, Draden {Drayden} Waters of CC, being very sick and weak in body, but of sound and disposing mind, memory and understanding;

To my three grandsons, James J. Turner, Alexander W. Turner and John C.C. Turner, 108 dollars and 75 cents, it being the balance

due me from Theophilus Dent for land rent which sum became due on the 8th day of November last and after debts applied to their education under direction of my daughter Kitty Turner.
Executor: daughter Kitty Turner
Signed: February 19, 1822   Draden Waters
Wit: William Matthews, Robert Davis

Page 259.
Reverend Charles Neale, Will,   November 27 1822; April 9, 1823
I, Charles Neale of CC, being sound in mind and understanding though somewhat infirm in body;
To Mechulda Boarman, now residing in the monastery in Charles County near Port Tobacco, all my real and personal estate to her and her heirs and appoint as Executrix. If she should die before me, then above mentioned property to Ann Mudd now residing in the monastery near Port Tobacco
Executor: Mechulda Boarman
Signed: November 27 1822   Charles Neale
Wit: John Matthews, John Edelen, James Brawner Jr. {recorded as Henry Brawner Jr. at probate}

Page 261.
Ann Maria Mitchell, Will,   May 21, 1822; January 7, 1823
I, Ann Maria Mitchell of CC, being of sound and disposing mind, memory and understanding;
To mother Elizabeth Mitchell, all my estate
Executrix: mother Elizabeth Mitchell
Signed: May 21, 1822   Ann M Mitchell
Wit: Francis Nelson, James D. Mitchell, James Roach
mm note: the will was dated May 21, 1823 in error if the probate is January 7, 1823

Page 263.
Vincent Posey, Will,   December 2, 1822; June 10, 1823
I, Vincent Posey of CC, being weak of body, but of a sound and disposing mind, memory and understanding;
Item: the whole of my estate real personal and mixed to be divided into 10 equal shares and distributed as follows:
   To wife Eleanor Posey, 1 share.
   To daughter Clarissa Dooley, 1 share.
   To son Harrison Posey, 1 share.
   To son Isaiah Posey, 1 share.
   To son Robert Harrison Posey, 1 share.

To son John Posey, 1 share.

To daughter Kitty Posey, 1 share and 100 dollars before distribution.

To daughter Elizabeth Posey, 1 share.

To son Zachariah Posey, 1 share.

To son Thomas Posey, 1 share.

Item: If my wife refuses to adhere to the above divisions and claim her proportions under law, then the residue of my estate after thirds are deducted shall be divided among the children in such manner and proportion as to give my children by the first marriage to wit; Hanson Posey, Clarissa Dooley, Isaiah Posey, Robert Hanson Posey, John Posey and Kitty Posey, the residue as may make each of their shares respectively the same as if she had agreed to the will, that is each of them shall have such an excess over and above the other three children as shall make their parts in the aggregate equal to six parts of the whole estate.

Executor: son Harrison Posey

Signed: December 2, 1822   Vincent Posey

Wit: John T. Stoddert, Thomas Dunnington, Truman Greenfield

Page 265.

Henrietta Wheeler, Will, July 29, 1822; June 11, 1823

I, Henrietta Wheeler of CC, being in perfect health of body, and of sound and disposing mind, memory and understanding;

To nephew Henry Jenkins, ½ share of my bank stock in the Bank of Columbia, which I deem to be 50 dollars.

To nephew John J. Jenkins, ½ share of the same bank stock.

To niece Mary Heard Jenkins, ½ share of the same bank stock.

To two nieces Grace Davis and Henrietta Jameson, ½ share of the same stock between them.

To niece Eleanor Edelen 1 full share of the same stock.

To niece Harriet Clarke, 100 dollars.

To Henrietta Kirk, 100 dollars and a bed and furniture.

To sister Mary Pye, 50 dollars.

To sister Mary Pye, 150 dollars out of which my funeral charges are to be paid and the balance to be applied to the repairs of St. Charles Church in Cornwallis Neck.

Executor: nephew John J. Jenkins

Signed: July 29, 1822   Henrietta Wheeler

Wit: Edward J. Heard, Joseph Edelen

Page 268.

Ann King Gray, Will, February 20, 1823; June 18, 1823

62

I, Ann King Gray of CC, being sick and weak of body, but of sound and
    disposing mind, memory and understanding;
To brother Benjamin Gray all my land to wit: part of "Wharton Manor"
    and "Eatons Delight", which we have an equal and undivided
    part. Also negroes; Bill, Betty, Frank, and Betty's two twins
    children Charity and Moses.
Executor: brother Benjamin Gray
Signed: February 20, 1823   Ann King Gray
Wit: Thomas H. Reeder, Uzziel Nalley, Otho Nalley

Page 269.
Nehemiah Franklin, Will,   June 15, 1823; August 2, 1823
I, Nehemiah Franklin of CC, being sick and weak in body, but of sound
    and disposing mind, memory and understanding;
To sister Priscilla Ratcliff, 100 dollars.
To Jane Ratcliff, d/o Robert Ratcliff, my riding mare.
To brother-in-law Robert Ratcliff, my saddle.
To my brother Thomas L.B. Franklin, my brothers-in-law Robert
    Ratcliff and Elkanah Franklin all the residue of my estate.
Executor: Walter M. Millar
Signed: June 15, 1823   Nehemiah Franklin
Wit: Isaac Bowie, Aeneas B. Allen, Caleb Pickarell

Page 271.
Joseph Barker, Will & Codicil June 10, 1823; August 19, 1823
To son Hezekiah Thomas Barker the plantation I bought of {Henry}
    Hendley McPherson called "Double Trouble" and "Double
    Trouble Englarged"; containing 360 acres. Also tract at Bean
    Town I bought of Eleanor Thompson containing 49 acres.
To daughter Kitty Ann Barker all the land that was deeded to her
    mother by Thomas I{saac} Reeves. Also tracts bought of Samuel
    Adams, being part of "Jordan" and "Charity" bought of Meveral
    Moran.
To son William Barker the plantation I now live on called Wardle" and
    "Wiltshire Plain" containing 490 acres. Also tracts "Drums Head"
    and "Second Mount Pleasant".
Item: the debt due me from Judson Hunt that is now in Charles County
    Court I leave to my son William.
Item: It is my will that my son William Barker will pay to my son
    Hezekiah Barker, the sum of 400 dollars to make him equal.
Item: my daughter Kitty Ann Barker shall pay to my son Hezekiah
    Thomas Barker, the sum of 300 dollars to make him equal.
Item: negroes Mary and Harriot and their children should be sold if

they misbehave.

Item: my three children, Hezekiah Thomas, Kitty Ann and William shall share and share alike in my personal property.

Executor: son Hezekiah Thomas Barker

Signed: June 10, 1823   Joseph Barker

Wit: Edward Turner, John W. McPherson, Judson Hunt, Jesse C. Cook

Codicil: I hereby revoke my appointment of my son Hezekiah Thomas Barker as executor and appoint Aquila Turner thereof.

Signed: August 1, 1823   Joseph Barker

Wit: Edward Turner, James Boarman, Roswell Harbin

Page 274.

George Gray, Will, February 23, 1823; August 20, 1823

I, George Gray of CC, being sick and weak in body, but of sound and disposing mind, memory and understanding;

To son John Gray and daughter Elizabeth Gray equally, the plantation whereon I now dwell, "Cedar Shelter", and a tract purchased of Raphael Boarman for which I have not obtained a deed.

To granddaughter Sophia Elizabeth Murdock, 1 cow and calf, 1 bed and furniture, and 100 dollars at 21 yrs.

To son John Gray and daughter Elizabeth Gray, 2 mares, 1 yoke of oxen with all my household stuff.

Item: I bequeath all the rest and residue of my personal estate divided among my three children, Mary Scott, John Gray and Elizabeth Gray.

Executor: son John Gray

Signed: February 23, 1823   George Gray

Wit: Richard Speake, Richard Brooke, William Rennor, Elizabeth W. Speake {Elizabeth Winter Dunnington?}

Page 277.

Henry Roberts, Will, August 1, 1823; August 20, 1823

I, Henry Roberts of CC;

To daughter Milly Ann Farrall, negro Maria (abt 16 yrs) and the sum of 25 dollars paid annually during her life.

To son Allison Roberts, negro William.

To four single daughters; Kitty Etheldra, Jane Christianna, Adaline and Rosetta Amanda and to my granddaughter Elizabeth R. Moore, seven negroes; Andrew, Ann, James, Benjamin, Lee, Leass and Spencer.

To son Allison and to my four single daughters; Kitty Etheldra, Jane Christianna, Adaline and Rosetta Amanda and to my granddaughter Elizabeth R. Moore all the lands I die possessed

64

of.
Executor: Allison Roberts
Signed: August 1, 1823   Henry Roberts
Wit: John N. Weems, William Hunt, John Boswell

Page 279.
Eleanor Margaret Brandt, Will,   July 27, 1823; August 30, 1823
I, Eleanor Margaret Brandt of CC;
To Aunt, Mary Kitty Weems, 1250 dollars.
To Aunt Anne B. Dent, 500 dollars.
To Ann Caroline Smoot, 1000 dollars
To brother Richard Hendley Brandt, negroes; James, Oscar and Mary,
and my gold watch.
To Miss Mary Griffin, 300 dollars
To Uncle Richard Brandt, 200 dollars
Executor: Uncle Wilson Smoot
Signed: August 30, 1823   Eleanor M. Brandt,
Wit: Jane F. Hargraves, John N. Weems
Then came James I. Weems and made oath ....
mm note: Jane F. Hargraves is Jane Fowke Hutchison.

Page 280.
Margaret Pye, Will,   October 28, 1820; August 19, 1823
I, Margaret Pye of CC, being sick and weak in body, but of sound and
    disposing mind, memory and understanding;
To my two daughters, Sarah Wright and Ann Reeder Nelson, negro
    Betty, and all her increase, but I reserve the use of Betty and one
    of her children, John Robert, to my daughter Anngelica Hudson
    during her natural life.
To daughter Sarah Wright, {negro} boys, Jim Sinker and Jack, 2 feather
    beds and furniture, 1 maple desk, 1 mahogany tea chest, 1 large
    hair trunk, 1 walnut table, 1 looking glass, all the horses of which
    I may die possessed of, and 2/3 of my other stock.
To daughter Ann Reeder Nelson, the remaining 1/3 of my stock and
    the use of negro woman Mary during her natural life and then to
    her children.
To grandson Ignatius Wright, the son of Joseph Wright dec'd 115
    pounds current money to be paid at 21yrs.
To my three daughters, Anngelica Hudson, Sarah Wright, and Ann
    Reeder Nelson, all the rest and residue of my estate
Executrixs: two daughters, Sarah Wright and Ann Reeder Nelson
Signed: October 28, 1820   Margaret Pye
Wit: Gowry Wright, Thomas Harrison Reeder, Abedrigo Posey

Page 283.

James Fenwick, Will December 3, 1823; October 21, 1823

I, James Fenwick of CC, being of sound and disposing mind and
memory;

To wife Teresa, all the negroes she brought me by marriage.

Item: In order to do away any dispute upon the question whether or
not old Mr. John Lancaster made a gift of negro Eleanor
commonly called Yellow Nell to my son Edward when an infant,
I hereby bequeath her and all her children to my son Edward
Fenwick.

Item: Whereas many years ago I sold to the deceased old Henry
Greenfield Sothoron of St. Mary's County, a tract of land lying in
{smudge} County the neighborhood of the town of Benedict
which I inherited as heir at law to my mother and I believe called
"Sinclair" or "Sinclair Resurveyed" and did give any bond for the
conveyance but owing that the papers having been mislaid or
lost, I have never given a deed of conveyance for the said land,
and whereas I have been informed that in the division of the
lands of the deceased Henry Greenfield Sothoron among his
children, the tract of land has fallen to his son Henry Sothoron. I
hereby bequeath to the said Henry Sothoron, all might right to
the aforesaid tract of land.

Item: Whereas among the stock in the bank of Columbia of George
Town and District of Columbia standing in my name, the amount
of 620 dollars is not really mine but was transferred to me in
trust only by Athanasius Fenwick as executor and in pursuance's
of the provisions of the last will and testament of my deceased
Aunt Mary Jenkins and as I do not know that I have any right or
power to appoint a successor to myself in said trust, it is my will
that in the event of my death before the final completion of the
trust that my executor shall transfer the amount of standing in
my name to such person to fulfill the ultimate intension and
disposition of my deceased Aunt Mary Jenkins.

To brother, the right Reverend Edward Fenwick, Bishop of Cincinnati
the sum of 100 dollars.

To grandson William Plowden Hamersley, all the lands I own in St.
Mary's County a part of which I bought of Ignatius Taney
deceased and have a deed of conveyance from his mother
Eleanor Taney, and the other part I bought of Raphael Taney
deceased. Should he die before 21 yrs, then to grandson Francis
Plowden. But it is nevertheless my will that my son-in-law
William H. Plowden and my daughter Henrietta Plowden have

the rents and profits of the said lands during their natural lives.

To grandson Robert James Brent, 1 lot or square of land in the City of Washington which I bought of Nicholas Young, but if he should die before 21 yrs, then to grandson William Brent.

To granddaughter Maria Brent, all the stock which I really own in the Bank of Columbia amounting somewhat upwards of 3100 dollars and appoint my son-in-law William L. Brent to be her guardian for the purpose of receiving the dividends during her minority.

Item: after these legacies and dispositions and my debts being paid, I give and bequeath to my wife Teresa all the remainder and residue of my real and personal estate during her natural life with the following exception that is to pay the sum of 400 dollars to my son Edward Fenwick for and during his natural life.

Item: after the death of my wife, I give and devise to my son-in-law Edmund [sic William L.] Plowden and my daughter Henrietta Plowden for and during their natural lives all my land lying above the round stone stand by Miss Anna Stoddert's and after their deaths to grandson Edmund Plowden.

Item: after the death of my wife, I give and devise to my son-in-law William L. Brent and my daughter Maryah during their natural lives all my land southwardly and westwardly or below the Stoddert's land including the tenement on which James Medley lives at the head of Pomonkey Creek and also including the land which I purchased of Benjamin F. Fendall and after their deaths to grandson Robert James Brent.

Executor: wife Teresa Fenwick

Signed: December 3, 1823   James Fenwick

Wit: Thomas D. Clagett, George Tennison, Thomas Lancaster

mm note: tract "Sinclair" was included in the resurvey of "Taney's Purchase", and located in Newport Hundred. James Fenwick was the eldest son of Ignatius Fenwick and Sarah Taney.

Page 288.

Benjamin Lomax, Will,   October 7, 1823; November 3, 1823

I, Benjamin Lomax of CC, being sick and weak in body, but in perfect sense disposing mind and memory;

To daughter Ann Lomax 1 bed and furniture.

To daughter Cecealy Meekins, the bed and furniture I now lye on.

To grandson James Terrell, my horse.

Item: the residue of my estate be divided into three equal parts; one to Ann Lomax, one to Sarah Terrell and the other to Elizabeth Ann Lomax widow of my deceased son Richard Lomax.

Executrixes: daughters Ann Lomax and Sarah Terrell

Signed: October 7, 1823   Benjamin Lomax
Wit: John W. Smoot, Charles Robey

Page 290.
Ann Rosella Middleton, Will, October 8, 1803; January 7, 1823
I, Ann Rosella Middleton of CC, being sick and weak of body, but of
    sound and disposing mind, memory and understanding;
To sister Lucretia Middleton, all my property both real and personal.
Executrix: sister Lucretia Middleton
Signed: October 8, 1803   Ann Rosella Middleton
Wit: Walter Baker Brooke, David Middleton, James H.A. Middleton
mm note: the date of will is written as "the eighth day of October in
    the year of our Lord eighteen hundred and three".

Page 292.
Jeremiah Dyer, Will, September 18, 1823; November 3, 1823
I, Jeremiah Dyer of CC, being sick and weak in body, but of sound and
    disposing mind, memory and understanding;
To wife Lucy Odre Dyer the whole of my property both real and
    personal to be disposed of as she may think proper.
Executrix: wife Lucy Odre Dyer
Signed: September 18, 1823   Jeremiah Dyer
Wit: James J. Reeves, Alexius Smith, William Queen

Page 293.
William Wheeler Lewis, Will, February 10, 1820; November 6, 1823
I, William W. Lewis of CC, being in perfect health of body, and of sound
    and disposing mind, memory and understanding;
To wife Elizabeth Tyer Lewis, my watch and locket and all jewelry that
    I heretofore bought her and also my wearing apparel at her
    disposal not to be sold.
To oldest son William Charles Lewis, my spy glass, quadain {quadrant}
    and sea books.
To son James Burgess Harper Lewis, my pistols.
To son George Washington Eugene Lewis, my sword that I lent to
    General Philip Stewart {Stuart}. Also 200 dollars.
To eldest daughter Mary Eleanor Lewis, 50 dollars.
To daughter Jane Lewis, 150 dollars.
To daughter Louise Elizabeth Lewis, 150 dollars.
To wife Elizabeth Tyer Lewis, all my silver of every description during
    her life and at her decease equally divided between my
    daughters.
Item: the rest and residue of my estate after my wife has taken her

thirds to my children.
Executor: wife Elizabeth Tyer Lewis
Signed: February 10, 1820   William Wheeler Lewis
Wit: Muncaster Moredock {Murdock}, Noble Barnes, John Adams

Page 295.
Mary Miles, Will,   December 7, 1822; November 6, 1823
I, Mary Miles of CC, being in a bad state of health, but of a sound and
      disposing mind;
To niece Rebeccah Cahoe, negroes; Teresa, Francis and Mary, 1 bed,
      bedstead and furniture.
To Henrietta Montgomery, a daughter of Francis Montgomery, 1 bed,
      bedstead and furniture.
To Benedict Joseph Montgomery, 1 cow and yearling.
To the presiding priest of the upper Zachia congregation, 10 dollars
      for masses.
To Rebeccah Cahoe the rest of my estate.
Executor: George Gardiner
Signed: December 7, 1822   Mary Miles
Wit: James Reeves, Henry L. Mudd

Page 297.
Maria King, Will,   March 30, 1821; November 15, 1823
I, Maria King of CC;
To Mrs. Barbara A. McPherson, a side board, the wife of Henry
      McPherson Sr.
To sisters Ann King, Margaret E. King and Leticia H. King
Executors: Henry McPherson Sr. and Edward Hamilton
Signed: March 30, 1821   Maria King
Wit: Morgan Harris, Stanislaus Coomes

Page 298.
Josiah Robey, Will,   November 1, 1823; November 24, 1823
I, Josiah Robey of CC, being sick and weak in body, but of sound and
      disposing mind, memory and understanding;
To sister Henrietta Bateman, living at present in Shepherds Town
      Virginia, 3000 dollars.
To sister Elizabeth Griffin, living at present in Tuscarora { Tuscarawas
      } County Ohio, 3000 dollars.
To sister Priscilla Sutherland living in Prince George's County
      Maryland, 3000 dollars.
To Allen Newton, my wearing apparel.
To nieces Catharine Mima Newton daughter of my deceased sister Ann

Newton, and Letty Jenkins daughter of my deceased sister
Martha Nalley, the rest and residue of my estate.
Executors: friends John Edelen and Henry Brawner
Signed: November 1, 1823   Josiah Robey
Wit: James Brawner Jr., Samuel Thompson

Page 300.
James Swann, Will,   October 26, 1817; January 12, 1824
In case of death my last will and desire is that my two children George
Swann and James Swann shall remain with their grandmother
and Aunt Rachel so long as they may wish to have them or until
necessary to send to school and they are not be separated
contrary to their wishes more than 3 months at one time and
John Leigh to have the management of all my business.
Executor: John Leigh
Signed: October 26, 1817   James Swann
Oath taken to the handwriting: William Holmes, Jesse Swann, Warren
Hobart

Page 301.
Elizabeth Smoot, Will,   October 6, 1823; January 12, 1824
I, Elizabeth Smoot late of Dorchester County Maryland, now a resident
of CC, being sick and weak of body, but of perfect and disposing
mind and memory;
To daughter Eliza Brawner, 1 pr shovel and tongs, 1 pr candle stands,
6 fruit spoons, all the earthen and china ware I have, 1 bed,
bedstead and furniture, 1 pair window curtains, 1 large chest.
Item: I ratify and confirm the bill of sale given to Basil Brawner for a
negro woman and child.
To son Joseph Smoot, 1 bed, bedstead and furniture.
To daughter Jane Robertson, all the articles left with her at my leaving
Dorchester County.
To son Thomas Smoot, all the articles left with him.
Item: all the money due me for rents, hires, etc., to be paid to my son
Joseph for the benefit of my son John W. Smoot under the
direction of my said son Joseph Smoot.
Executor: none nominated
Signed: October 6, 1823   Elizabeth Smoot
Wit: Daniel Kennedy, Patrick C. Murray

Page 303.
Joanna Truman Stoddert, Will,   January 18, 1824; January 27, 1824
I, Joanna Truman Stoddert of CC, being in a weak state of health, but

of sound and disposing mind, memory and understanding;

To Joanna Edgar Ward, ½ my real and personal estate.

To Joanna Stoddert McPherson and Henry Middleton Brawner the other ½.

Executor: Doctor William McPherson

Signed: January 18, 1824   Joanna Truman Stoddert

Wit: Thomas D. Clagett, Edward Fenwick, Robert Fenwick

Page 305.

Elizabeth King, Will,   February 13, 1821; February 7, 1824

This is the last will and testament of Elizabeth King of CC;

To sister of Letitia H. King, negro Dick.

To Reverend Charles Neale, 100 dollars.

To my three sisters, Ann King, Maria King and Margaret E. King, the residue of my estate.

Executors: Henry McPherson of Henry, Doctor George A. Carroll

Signed: February 13, 1821   Elizabeth King

Wit: Sarah Ann Coomes, Joseph Green

Page 306.

William Turner Sr., Will,   January 3, 1824; February 23, 1824

I, William Turner of CC, being infirm of body, but of sound mind and memory;

To wife Mary Turner, all my property real and personal to dispose of as she may think best.

Executrix: wife Mary Turner

Signed: January 3, 1824   William Turner Sr.

Wit: Thomas Martin, John W. McPherson, John H. Thomas

Page 308.

Elizabeth Posey, Will,   September 2, 1823; March 1, 1824

I, Elizabeth Posey of CC, being sick and weak of body, but of sound and disposing mind, memory and understanding;

To three nephews, William Dixon, George Dixon and Noble Dixon, my 3 beds, bedsteads and furniture. Also the rest and residue of my estate except 300 dollars which I loaned my brother John Dixon of which I leave him clear.

To nephew George Dixon, 6 silver tea spoons.

Executor: brother John Dixon

Signed: September 2, 1823   Elizabeth Posey

Wit: Ignatius F. Clements, Pamelia Dixon

Page 309.
Thomas Yates Robey, Will,   May 11, 1824; May 25, 1824
I, Thomas Yates Robey of CC, being sick and weak in body, but of sound and disposing mind, memory and understanding;
To two cousins, Isaiah Robey and Precious Robey, all my real estate to have an hold so long as my cousin Precious Robey remains single and at her marriage the whole of my real estate to my cousin Isaiah Robey.
To cousin Isaiah Robey all my personal estate consisting of 1 bed and furniture, household and kitchen furniture.
Executor: none nominated
Signed: May 11, 1824   Thomas Y. Robey
Wit: Elisha Robey, Catharine Robey, William Morton

Page 310.
Thomas Milstead, Will,   October 8, 1818; May 12, 1824
I, Thomas Milstead of CC, being sick and weak in body, but of sound and disposing mind, memory and understanding;
To eldest son Matthew Milstead all the land devised to me by my father, known by the name of the "Two Loving Brothers" whereon Walter Warden now lives to him the said Matthew Milstead his heirs and assigns in fee simple.
To two sons Ignatius Milstead and Thomas Milstead the plantation whereon I now live know by the name of "Williams Purchase", "Garner's Addition", and one other tract or parcel of land joining which I bought of Benjamin Gray's heirs.
To daughter Margaret Haislep one negroe the choice out of my negroes, one cow and one feather bed and one furniture.
To daughter Frances Fugett {Fugate} one negroe the second choice out of my negroes.
To daughter Eleanor Milstead one negro the third choice of my negroes and one cow & one feather bed & furniture.
To daughter Sarah Garner, one negro the fourth choice out of my negroes and feather bed and furniture and one cow and no more of my estate.
Item: whereas my daughter Elizabeth hath greatly displeased me by her conduct I therefore shall give her nothing.
Item I give and bequeath all the balance of my property of whatever it may consist, to my sons Matthew Milstead, Ignatius Milstead and Thomas Milstead and my daughters Margaret Haislep, Frances Fugett {Fugate} and Eleanor Milstead to be equally divided between them, with the exception, that Ignatius Milstead and Thomas Milstead to have out of this last clause of this will one

cow and bed and furniture each more than the rest and it is my wish and desire that there shall be no administration on my estate, but that my property may divided agreeable to this my request.

Executors: sons Ignatius Milstead and Thomas Milstead
Signed: October 8, 1818   Thomas Milstead
Wit: Francis E. Dunnington, Joseph Davis, Richard Milstead

Page 311.
Edward Hamilton Sr., Will,   May 11, 1824; June 8, 1824
I, Edward Hamilton Sr. of CC, being sound in mind though infirm in body;

To son Edward I. Hamilton, his choice of my two plantations, that which I now reside, commonly called "Prospect Hill" and of my plantation being a part of "Causins Manor" and "Wathens Adventure" whereon my son now resides. If he chooses the plantation he now resides on, then I bequeath to him 20- acres of timbered land in Zachiah Swamp, part of my plantation "Prospect Hill".

To daughter Ann Catharine Hamilton all the remaining plantation after my son declares his choice.

To Mechulda Boarman now residing in the monastery near Port Tobacco the sum of 700 dollars.

Item: I will and order a Sunday suit of clothes to be given to each of my working slaves together with a hat.

To my two children, Edward I. Hamilton and Ann Catharine Hamilton, the residue of my estate, real or personal.

Executor: son Edward I. Hamilton
Signed: May 11, 1824   Edward Hamilton Sr.
Wit: Samuel Hawkins, Josias H. Hawkins, Benedict Fenwick

Page 315.
James Moore, Will,   May 20, 1824; June 9, 1824
I, James Moore of CC, being infirm in body, but sound in mind, memory and understanding;

To wife Elizabeth Moore, all my property both real and personal
Executors: wife Elizabeth Moore and Doctor William Queen
Signed: May 20, 1824   James Moore
Wit: Samuel Adams, Hugh Murray, John Boswell

Page 317.
William Hollis, Will (copy),   July 22, 1819; January 6, 1824
I, William Hollis of Hartford County Maryland, being of a sound

disposing mind, memory and understanding;

To son James Hollis, negro Sarah now in his possession with the bible I left with him.

To daughter Mary Webster, 100 dollars and her two sons William and Augustus, 1000 dollars and I will that my Bush River Neck farm remain rented and the rent be paid them till they are paid off.

To granddaughter Sarah Frances Webster, negro Bell.

To granddaughter Mary F. Webster, negro Sophia.

To daughter Mary Webster, negro Robert, but if my son John Hollis will pay her 300 dollars then I will said Robert to him.

To daughter Sarah Day, negro Minta and my sorrel mare and 200 dollars to be paid her from the rent of my farm on Pacas Park [Gunpowder Upper and Gunpowder Lower Hundred}.

To granddaughter Milsha A. Day, negro Ellen.

To granddaughter Priscilla Day, negro Caroline.

To grandson James Day, negro Charles and 6 mahogany chairs.

To daughter Frances Hollis, negroes, Hinny, Myls, Isaac, Eliza and Phillis Ann, and my bay mare I bought of James Hollis, and such of my bedding now in her possession, my mahogany tea tables, 200 cord of wood off my land of Pacas Park. Nevertheless, If my son Richard F. Hollis will pay my daughter 600 dollars within three years of my death, then negro Isaac and wood to said son.

To son Richard Frisby Hollis, negroes, Harry, Hannah and the use of all my farm on Pacas Park during his life with liberty to cut 1/3 of all the wood except chestnut and what is before willed, which he is only to use for fencing and building on the farm, on the east side of the main road leading to Otter Point.

To son Alonzo Hollis, all my houses and lotts in Alingdon and all my lots of land on the west side of the main road leading to Otter Point, viz, two lots, one I bought of Pacas and Baker and deeded to me by Richard Dallam trustee , and one lot called the "Cool Spring" I bought of John P. Paca. Also all my land in Bush River Neck. If son dies without issue, then the houses and lots to Mary Webster during her life and after her life to her son William, and my Bush River Neck lands to my son John Hollis. {long conditional instructions follow if sons Richard, Alonzo or John die w/o issue}. Also negroes; Abram and George Washington.

To son John Hollis, all my lands in Charles County I bought of Philip Stewart {Stuart}, and all my right to the land I bought of William Dye and all my seins and battoes [sic] provided he pay my debts to Philip Stewart for the land.

Item: I will that my son John Hollis sell my negroes Harry and Peter to pay what I owe in Alexandria and what I owe to James Hollis. I also will my son John have my negroes Frank and Sealak by paying 200 dollars and the monies paid applied to my debts.

Item: I will that my son Richard F. Hollis executor of my estate in Somerset and Harford Counties and my son John Hollis to be executor in Charles County.

To sons Richard, John and Alonzo Hollis all my lands in Somerset to be equally divided.

Executor: sons Richard F. Hollis and John Hollis

Signed: July 22, 1819   William Hollis

Wit: William Allen, William Bradford, Daniel Kendrick, Robert T. Allen

Certified by Thos. S. Bond R.W.HCy

Maryland Sct. I hereby certify that the within and foregoing is a true transcript from the original recorded in the office of the Register of Wills for Harford County. In testimony whereof I have hereunto set my hand and affixed the seal of my office this 12ᵗʰ day of January 1824. Thomas S Bond R.W.HCy

mm note: William Hollis/Holles, MSA S 1218-200, Unpatented Certificate 194 {to resurvey Woodburys Harbour Sep 26, 1817 located on the Potomac River}, 1818/08/15, Harbour Secured, 177 Acres, 2 Rods. This certificate can be viewed at:

Page 1:
http://msa.maryland.gov/megafile/msa/stagser/s1200/s1218/000 200/000200/tif/dsl00200-1.jpg

Page 2:
http://msa.maryland.gov/megafile/msa/stagser/s1200/s1218/000 200/000200/tif/dsl00200-2.jpg

Page 3:
http://msa.maryland.gov/megafile/msa/stagser/s1200/s1218/000 200/000200/tif/dsl00200-3.jpg

Page 4:
http://msa.maryland.gov/megafile/msa/stagser/s1200/s1218/000 200/000200/tif/dsl00200-4.jpg

1642-1753 Rent Rolls Charles County MD Hundred - Riverside: Rent Roll, page/Sequence: 346-24: Woodsberry Harbour: 300 acres; Possession of - 300 Acres - Lampton, Mark: Surveyed 27 July 1667 for James Lee on the North Side Potomac river near a march called the half way between Maryland Point and Nanjemoy Creek this land was vested in John Hitchinson who died without heir. Whereby it came to be escheated to his Lordship and granted John Allen who assigned the same to John Fanning & patent in Fanning name 1677 yearly rent.

Page 321.
William McAtee, Will, April 26, 1824; August 11, 1824
I, William Macatee of CC, being weak in health but of sound and
    disposing mind, memory and understanding;
To brother Henry McAtee, all my personal and real estate.
Executor: brother Henry McAtee
Signed: April 26, 1824   W. McAtee
Wit: Benedict I. Jenkins, Eliza Jenkins, Charles I. Lancaster

Page 322.
Middleton Meek Rison, Will, September 16, 1820; August 11, 1824
I, Middleton M. Risin of CC, being of sound and disposing mind and
    memory;
To brother Peter Risin, 2 dollars.
To Margaret Resin, 2 dollars.
To John R. Evans, the entire balance of my estate.
Executor: John R. Evans
Signed: September 16, 1820   Middleton M. Risin
Wit: William Brawner of Edward, Teresa Brawner, William Posey

Page 324.
Martha Dent, Will, July 4, 1816; August 10, 1824
I, Martha Dent of CC, being sick and weak in body, but of sound and
    disposing mind, memory and understanding;
To son Wilfred Dent five negroes; Moses, Stephen, Alice, Pam and
    Robert.
To daughter Ann Dent eight negroes; Gustavus, Terry, Mary, Eliza,
    George, Watt, Hanson and Allen.
To granddaughter Lucinda E. Dent two negroes; Minta and Sandy.
To granddaughter Emily Matthews negro Mark.
To son Wilfred Dent and daughter Ann Dent, all the rest and residue
    of property equally.
Executor: son Wilfred Dent
Signed: July 4, 1816   Martha Dent
Wit: Alexander Dent, John B.E. Dent, John T. Dent
Charles County Sct. The within and aforegoing instrument of writing
    being exhibited into court and it appearing to the court that
    Wilfred Dent the Executor is absent from the state and beyond
    the reach of their process it is therefore ordered that with a view
    to the perpetuation of evidence of the subscribing witnesses
    thereto, the said instrument of writing be admitted to probate.

Page 326.

William Sheirburn, Will, November 23, 1823; August 16, 1824

I, William Sheirburn of CC, being of sound and perfect mind and memory;

To brother Joseph Sheirburn all my personal estate.

Executor: brother Joseph Sheirburn

Signed: November 23, 1823   William Sheirburn

Wit: Josias H. Hawkins {the second witness did not appear and the name left blank. It appears to be a Latin phrase}

Page 327.

Wilfred Manning, Will & Codicil, May 12, 1821; September 22, 1824

I, Wilfred Manning of CC, being of perfect mind and memory;

Imprimis; my body to be plainly buried at the monastery in Charles County.

To the Reverend Gentlemen that may officiate at Saint Thomas Church, 30 dollars to have masses said for me.

To wife Dorothy Manning, 1/3 part of my personal estate with my carriage and horses alone.

To daughter Catharine H. Manning, 100 dollars only because she is provided for better than I can provide for her.

To daughter Ann Charlotte Young, who I consider better off than the rest of my children, and I have given her some property heretofore, 100 dollars.

To sons John Alexander Manning and Alonzo M. Manning the rest and residue of my estate real and personal. And that when the lands are divided, the dwelling house and out houses shall be given to Alonzo M. Manning and he to give his mother a home in the dwelling house during her natural life.

Item: it also enters into my view in dividing my real estate that I have expended a considerable sum in the education of John Alexander Manning and Alonzo M. Manning remains to be educated.

Executrix: wife Dorothy Manning

Signed: May 12, 1821   Wilfred Manning

Wit: Charles A. Pye, Nicholas Stonestreet, Lewis Stonestreet

Codicil:

Since the execution of my will, I have purchased a tracts of land from George Dyer and Theodore Mudd, which shall be divided equally between my two sons John Alexander Manning and Alonzo M. Manning.

I will that my wife Dorothy Manning shall keep all my lands, stock and negroes, etc, together for four years from the first day of January next, and to apply the proceeds toward paying of my just debts.

Then the property, real and personal to be divided, and if son Alonzo M. Manning elects not to live in the dwelling house with his mother, then the executrix shall pay to him annually 200 dollars.
Signed: August 30, 1824   Wilfred Manning
Wit: Nicholas Stonestreet, Charles A. Pye, Robert Digges

Page 331.
Elizabeth Jenifer, Will, July 8, 1824; no probate date
I, Elizabeth Jenifer of CC, being at this time in a weak and low state of health, but of perfectly sound mind, memory and understanding;
To friend Henry Brawner Esquire Attorney at Law, the whole of my landed estate and my negroes {in trust}; Polly, Levy and Joseph after my debts and subject to pay on account of my having been security for my brother John Winter and to use and apply the profits and benefits arising from the said landed estate and the use and labour of the negroes for the support and maintenance of my brother John Winter during his life or for his children if he should have any. In case of my brother's death without lawful heir, hold the lands and negroes for the use and benefit for the children of Daniel Jenifer.
To Ann Orphelia Jenifer, daughter of Daniel Jenifer, negro Mary Ann, and my gold watch.
To John Campbell Jenifer son of Daniel Jenifer, negro Walbert.
To Daniel of St. Thomas Jenifer son of Daniel Jenifer, negro Samuel son of my negro Mary.
To Marian Eliza Jenifer daughter of Daniel Jenifer, negro Mary daughter of Jenny Lee.
To John Campbell Jenifer and Marian Eliza Jenifer, negro Sall and her two children in compliance of a promise that I made to their grandmother Mrs. Marian Campbell.
To negro Judith Cruck, to be free and discharged from slavery and request Daniel Jenifer to build her a house on the land and give her 10 dollars and 3 barrels of Indian corn yearly.
Item: I discharge John Campbell from the payment of any money which he may owe me.
Item: should there be any money left after debts, it to be held in trust by my executor for the use and benefit of Mrs. Marian Campbell.
To cousin Elizabeth Trippe Jenifer and Daniel Jenifer, all the rest of my property
Executor: Daniel Jenifer
Signed: July 8, 1824   Eliza Jenifer
Wit: William Latimer, Samuel Latimer, Marcus L. Adderton

78

Page 335.
George Dyer, Will, October 6, 1823; October 19, 1824
I, George Dyer of CC, being sick and weak in body, but of sound and
    disposing mind, memory and understanding;
To wife Dorothy Dyer all my estate both real and personal to be
    disposed as she may deem proper.
Executrix: wife Dorothy Dyer
Signed: October 6, 1823   George Dyer
Wit: George Gardiner, A.J.P. Boarman {or A.T.P}, Jeremiah Dyer

Page 336.
John Dixon, Will, September 5, 1824; October 1, 1824
I, John Dixon of CC, being sick of body, but of sound and disposing
    mind, memory and understanding;
To wife 1/3 and the balance equally divided between all my children.
Executor: son-in-law Ignatius F. Clements
Signed: September 5, 1824   John Dixon
Wit: Edward J. Heard, Alfred Berry

Page 337.
John Perry, Will, September 9, 1822; November 18, 1824
I, John Perry of CC, being sick and weak in body, but of sound and
    disposing mind, memory and understanding;
To wife Elizabeth Perry, all the lands I now own during her natural life
    and then to my son J.B. Perry.
To son J.B. Perry, choice, 1 negro, 1 horse and 1 bed and furniture at
    the death of my wife.
To wife Elizabeth Perry the use and profits, hires and interest of my
    personal estate during her natural life or widowhood and then
    disposed among my four daughters after my son's legacy is taken
    as follows; to youngest daughters Catharine Jane Perry, Judith
    Ann Perry and Elizabeth Perry a legacy out of my personal estate
    to make their share equal to which I have heretofore given to my
    daughter Margaret Elizabeth Price.
Executors: wife Elizabeth Perry and son J.B. Perry
Signed: September 9, 1822   John Perry
Wit: Nathan Dunnington, Giles J. Perry, John F. Dunnington

Page 339.
Henry McAtee, Will, November 10, 1824; November 18, 1824
I, Henry Macatee of CC, being weak in health, but of sound and
    disposing mind and memory;
First: it is my will and desire that all my just debts due from my

deceased brother William McAtee and myself should be paid.
Secondly, the remaining part of my estate real and personal, be divided as follows; 2/3 to my niece Sarah Ann Edelen and 1/3 to John Henry Edelen her brother.
Executor: William H. Neale
Signed: November 10, 1824   Henry McAtee
Wit: B.J. Jenkins, Michael Boarman, Charles J. Lancaster

Page 340.
Malachi Robey, Will,   September 12, 1824; November 21, 1824
I, Malachi Robey of CC, being sick and weak of body, but of sound mind, memory and understanding;
To wife Mary Robey, negroes; Thomas, Candas and Eliza, 1 yoke of oxen and 1 cart, 1 sorrel mare, 1 grey horse, 1 brindle cow, 1 brindle cow with white face, 1 bed and furniture.
To son Francis Robey, negroes; Abednigo and Caroline.
To son Henry Malachi Robey, negroes; Richard and Delia.
To son Samuel Carrington Robey, negroes; Nathan Thomasand Sarah.
To daughter Elizabeth Robey, negroes; Mary and Hanson.
To daughter Martha Robey, negroes; Maria and her child John Henry, and Basil Thomas s/o Harriet.
To daughter Ann Robey, negroes; Celia and Jane the d/o Maria, and 50 dollars.
To daughter Mary Eleanor Robey, negroes; Harrison and Harriet.
Item: all the residue of my estate equally divided between my wife and seven children as before named.
Executor: son Francis Robey
Signed: September 12, 1824   Malachi Robey
Wit: Elias Robey, Rezin A. Boswell

Page 342.
Barbara Ann McPherson, Will,   September 25, 1824; November 29, 1824
I, Barbara Ann McPherson of CC, being sick and weak of body, but of sound and disposing mind and memory;
To two sons, John Henry McPherson and Samuel Chapman McPherson all by real and personal estate reserving to my husband Henry McPherson their father a genteel and comfortable maintenance at the discretion of my nephew John G. Chapman who I appoint my Executor
Executor: nephew John G. Chapman
Signed: September 25, 1824   Barbara Ann McPherson
Wit: Joseph Green, William P. Ford, William McPherson

Page 343.
Thomas Robey, Will,   June 6, 1824; November 30, 1824
I, Thomas Robey of CC, being of sound and disposing mind, memory
and understanding;
To grandson William Thomas Robey, part of tracts "Robey's Range"
containing 146 acres, and "Robey's Beginnings" containing 34-½
acres, on condition he give up all claim to the 350 dollars which
I am indebted to him.
To son John N. Robey, tract "Griffins Seat" containing 94-1/4 acres,
also negro Arey.
To grandson Peter H. Robey, negro Andrew.
To granddaughter Sarah Ann Robey, part of tract "Robey's Range"
containing 104 acres and 1 acre of land out of tract "Robey's
Beginning" to be laid off according to certain stones fixed by me
as the divisional line between her and her brother William
Thomas Robey. The above lands are given in lieu of and in bar of
the 350 dollars which I am indebted to her.
To daughter Matilda Hunt, negro Mary.
Executor: grandson Isaiah Robey
Signed: June 6, 1824   Thomas Robey
Wit: Alexander Matthews, Peter Robey, Elias Robey

Page 345.
Kitty McPherson, Will,   1824; December 15, 1824
To brother Thomas McPherson, negro George, my dining table,
looking glass, 2 decanters and bed and two counterpanes.
To nephew George Washington Garner, negro Cy.
To Aunt Catherine McPherson, 50 dollars.
To two nephews Samuel William Hanson McPherson and Edmond
Suttland McPherson all the rest of my property.
To my sister Elizabeth McPherson, a mourning ring with some of my
hair.
Executor: brother Thomas McPherson
Signed: 1824   not signed
Oath that will was in deceased handwriting: William McPherson

Page 346.
Meverel Moran, Will,   August 2, 1821; February 9, 1825
I, Meverel Moran of CC, being in perfect health of body, and of sound
and disposing mind, memory and understanding;
To son Thomas Alfred Moran, all the whole of my estate real and
personal, and if he should die without lawful heir or before 20
yrs old, then to my four nieces, Mary Wood, Susan Wood, Ann

Wood, Jane Wood.
Executor: son Thomas Alfred Moran
Signed: August 2, 1821   Meverel Moran
Wit: William Morton, Clement J. Billingsly, Henry Canter

Page 348.
Kitty Ann Thomas, Will, September 27, 1824; February 19, 1825
I, Kitty Ann Thomas of CC, being weak of body, but of perfect mind and
     memory;
To mother Priscilla Thomas, all my property both real and personal
Executor: mother Priscilla Thomas
Signed: September 27, 1824   Kitty Ann Thomas
Wit: Thomas Martin, Joshua Estep, Jane S. Estep

Page 349.
Robert Taylor, Will, February 7, 1825; March 5, 1825
I, Robert Taylor of CC, being sick and weak of body, but of sound mind,
     memory and understanding;
To wife Mary Ann Taylor, in addition to the property already secured
     to her by marriage contract, 1 horse, 1 cow, bed with furniture, 1
     square dining table of cherry wood, chests, all the earthenware,
     knives, forks, spoons and glasses such as drinking glasses, and
     100 dollars cash.
To three daughters, Virlinda Martin, Eleanor Speake and Mary Taylor,
     all the residue of my personal estate.
Executor: son-in-law Doctor Thomas Martin
Signed: February 7, 1825   Robert Taylor
Wit: John W. Smoot, Walter M. Millar, Thomas Perry, Harriet Posey

Page 352.
Robert Halkerston, Will, June 17, 1824; March 7, 1825
I, Robert Halkerston of CC, being of sound disposing mind and
     memory;
To wife Malinda Halkerston all that is due me from my brother
     William Halkerston's esate together will all and every article I
     may possess at my demise, and after her life, to my son-in-law
     Walter Baker Boswell.
Executor: wife Malinda Halkerston
Signed: June 17, 1824   Robert Halkerston
Wit: John W. Smoot, Mary Scroggin

[page intentionally blank]

INDEX

William, 51, 54, 75, 79
McConchie
  Alexander Jones, 15
  Thomas, 15
McCubbin
  Elizabeth Hanson Fendall, 37
McEldery
  Elizabeth, 38
  Horatio C., 13, 38
  Hugh, 38
  John Patrick, 38
  Mary Elizabeth, 38
McMillan
  Hugh, 39
McPherson
  Barbara A., 68
  Barbara Ann, 79
  Catherine, 80
  Edmond Suttland, 80
  Elishabah B., 36, 37
  Elizabeth, 80
  Elizabeth Margaret Hanson, 36
  Henry, 42, 68, 70, 79
  Henry} Hendley, 62
  Joanna Stoddert, 70
  John W., 20, 63, 70
  Kitty, 80
  Samuel Chapman, 79
  Samuel William Hanson, 80
  Thomas, 80
  William, 70, 79, 80
McWilliams
  Elizabeth, 49
Medley
  James, 66
Meek
  Catharine T., 11, 14
  Catharine T{aliaferro}, 14
  Joseph H., 14
  Richard B., 14

Meekins
  Cecealy, 66
Meredith
  John, 15
Merrick
  William D., 24, 48
  William D{uhurst}, 24
Middleton
  Ann Rosella, 67
  David, 67
  E.A., 24
  James H.A., 67
  Lucretia, 67
  Mary Ann Dent Ireland, 11, 14
  Taliaferro Hooe, 14
Miles
  Joseph, 49
  Mary, 68
Millar
  Alexander, 27
  Ann Maria, 27
  Walter M., 19, 27, 62, 81
Mills
  Nicholas, 53
Milstead
  Eleanor, 71
  George K., 22
  Ignatius, 71, 72
  Matthew, 71
  Richard, 72
  Thomas, 42, 71, 72
Mitchell
  Ann Maria, 27, 60
  Elizabeth, 27, 60
  James D., 60
  James W., 27
Monroe
  Ann, 12
  Mary, 12
  Sarah, 12
  Sophia, 12

John, 28
Kitty Etheldra, 63
Rosetta Amanda, 63
Robertson
Catharine, 33, 34
George, 22, 33, 34, 44
Gerard, 15
Jane, 69
Robey
Alexander, 5, 28, 44
Ann, 31, 79, 80
Asseneth, 5
Baruch, 28
Cassandra, 28
Catharine, 28, 71
Charles, 67
Chloe, 28
Eleanor, 5
Elias, 28, 79, 80
Elisha, 5, 40, 71
Eliza, 28
Elizabeth, 44, 79
Francis, 79
Henry, 44
Heshijah {Hezekiah}, 28
Horace, 28
Isaiah, 71, 80
James Wilson, 44
John, 5
John A., 40
John Acton, 5
John N., 80
Josiah, 68, 69
Judith, 44
Lucy, 28
Malachi, 79
Malinda, 44
Martha, 79
Mary, 44, 79
Mary Eleanor, 79
Nancy, 5
Peter, 80

Peter H., 80
Precious, 71
Samuel Carrington, 79
Sarah, 28
Theodore, 5
Thomas, 80
Thomas Yates, 71
Uriah, 44
Virlinder, 5
William Thomas, 28, 80
Robinson
Hezekiah W., 13
James, 27
Rowe
George, 41
George Marlow, 41
John, 40, 41
Mary Ann, 41
Polly J., 41
Sarah Elizabeth, 41
Sanders
Ann Margaret, 23
John F.R., 23
Matilda Margaret Snowden, 27
Sangster
Alexander, 26
Sansberrie
Isadore, 26
Thomas B., 26, 27
Saunders
Sarah Elizabeth S., 23
Scott
Levi, 51, 52
Mary, 63
Richard M., 18
Scrivner
Thomas, 56
Scroggin
Jane, 18
Mary, 83
Walter, 18

Stewart
  Francis Ignatius, 54
  Philip, 67, 73
  William, 37, 38
Stoddert
  Anna, 66
  Joanna Truman, 69, 70
  John T., 61
Stone
  David, 30
Stonestreet
  Charles Henry, 9
  Henry, 9
  Joseph N., 11
  Joseph Noble, 9
  Lewis, 9, 76
  Mary E., 9
  Mary Noble, 9
  Nicholas, 3, 9, 76, 77
Storer
  Dorothy H., 18
Storke
  Johannis Greenfield Dent, 13
Stout
  Ebeneazer, 19
Stuart
  James, 38
  John, 38
  Richard, 11
  William, 37, 38
Summers
  Jane, 22
Sutherland
  Priscilla, 68
Swann
  Catharine C., 44
  Elkanah, 56
  George, 69
  James, 69
  Jesse, 69
  Richard R., 23

Sweny
  Allen, 15
Talburtt
  George Washington, 47
Taney
  Eleanor, 65
  Ignatius, 65
  Raphael, 65
  Sarah, 66
Taylor
  John, 34
  Mary, 81
  Mary Ann, 81
  Robert, 81
Tennison
  George, 66
Terrell
  James, 66
  Sarah, 66
Thomas
  Jesse, 32, 33
  John H., 31, 70
  Kitty Ann, 81
  Priscilla, 81
Thompson
  Ann, 30
  Eleanor, 62
  James, 29
  Samuel, 69
  William, 18
Thorn
  Jane, 46
  William, 13
Thornton
  George F., 11
Tiar
  William A., 23, 32
Tier
  Charles A., 32
Townshend
  Daniel, 22

106

Wheeler
  Ann, 19, 24
  Barbary, 35
  Clement, 19
  Darkey {Dorcas}, 44
  Edward, 35, 36
  Elizabeth, 35
  Hennariettar, 35
  Henrietta, 19, 61
  James, 44
  Josias, 35
  Luke, 19
  Mary, 19
  William, 19
Wilder
  Rebeccah, 39
Williams
  Margaret, 31
Wills
  Charles, 51
  Jane, 51
  Joseph J., 55
  Lucy Ann, 55
  Maria, 55
Wilson
  Elizabeth, 44
Winter
  Eliza, 39
  John, 38, 77
  William H., 11

Wiseman
  William, 26
Wood
  Ann, 22, 23, 31, 32, 43, 81
  Ferdinand F., 23, 32
  George L., 23
  Giles C., 23
  Giles G., 31, 32
  Henry S., 23
  Ignatius, 22, 32, 51
  Jane, 81
  Mary, 80
  Susan, 80
  William B., 32
  William S., 23
Woodward
  Ann, 2
Woodyear
  Elizabeth Rachel, 2
Wright
  Gowry, 64
  Ignatius, 64
  John W., 14, 22
  Joseph, 22, 64
  Sarah, 64
Yates
  Henry S., 57
  Judith, 39
Young
  Ann Charlotte, 76
  Noble, 43
  Sarah, 41, 42

TESTATOR INDEX
(the page number refers to the page in the original will book HB-14)

Surname	First Name	Second	Page
Baily	John		13
Barker	Joseph		271
Beaven	Benjamin		111
Beaven	Mary		26
Beaven	Walter		16
Berry	Hezekiah		199
Berry	Prior		109
Blacklock	Nicholas	Frederick	34
Boarman	Aloysius		148
Bond	Thomas		89
Bond	Walter		38
Bowling	Jeremiah		31
Bowling	Mary		145
Brandt	Eleanor Margaret		279
Brawner	Esther		246
Brawner	Henry	Sr.	178
Brawner	Thomas	S.	194
Bruce	Robert		81
Campbell	Catharine		164
Canter	Eleanor		226
Carrington	John	E.	123
Cawood	Mary	Fendall	152
Clements	John	Adler	52
Clements	Richard	B.	78
Clements	Thomas	C.	249
Coffer	John		156
Collins	Samuel		243
Contee	Jane		120
Cooke	John	W.	135
Cooke	William	Sr.	76

110

114

www.ingramcontent.com/pod-product-compliance
Lightning Source LLC
Chambersburg PA
CBHW071229290326
41931CB00037B/2533